My friend Tina Konkin experienced ⌐ ⌐ ⌐
marriage. Divorce could have been the end of her story, but
instead, through prayer, hard work, and a powerful dose
of God's redemptive grace, she and her husband emerged
from that crisis with a deeper and stronger relationship
than they had known before. Now Tina has dedicated her
life to ministering to couples in crisis and helping them
find healing and renewal—a mission we heartily embrace
at Focus on the Family. If your marriage is at a breaking
point, this book can help.

GREG SMALLEY, PSY.D.
Vice president, Marriage and Family Formation, Focus on the Family

This courageous story of brokenness and betrayal reveals
how God can bring hope and restoration in the midst of
marital devastation. Journey with Tina and her husband,
Ron, through their struggle to learn and apply the healing
principles they discovered while rebuilding their marriage
with compassion and forgiveness. Their Relationship Lifeline
ministry has breathed new life into hundreds of marriages,
including many in my own church family. For anyone
experiencing the pain of betrayal, I encourage you to grab hold
of Tina's story and trust Jesus to transform your relationships
into something more than you could ever imagine.

MATTHEW CORK
Senior pastor, Friends Church Yorba Linda, and superintendent,
Evangelical Friends Church, Southwest Region

This book is a treasure. Everyone needs this book or knows
someone who needs it. Tina courageously invites us into
her story to learn from her journey. She has filled this
book with godly wisdom and insight on how to take steps

to move forward in life. As pastors, we are committed to seeing marriages, families, and relationships thrive, and we consider it an honor and privilege to support and endorse this book and the work and ministry of Tina Konkin.

JOHN AND HELEN BURNS
Pastors, Relate Church, Canada

Tina passed through order (a secure marriage) to chaos (infidelity) and back to order (restored marriage) and then chaos (widowhood). This is a remarkable story of choosing to let the power of love conquer all.

DR. CAROLINE LEAF
Cognitive neuroscientist

Here's *the* book on radical relationship restoration for a throwaway society. This book comes not from the voice of theorists but from hardcore practitioners. Tina and her late husband, Ron, challenged so many couples to face the fractured facts of life with faith, hope, love, brutal courage, and even a sense of humor. This is not a book for the faint of heart, escapists, or blame- and shame-based reactionaries. Read it—and prepare to rewrite the story of your life.

GORDON RIDDLE PENNINGTON
Founder, Burning Media Group

Pastors see many marriages go through challenges and hardships, but betrayal is perhaps the most deadly, destructive force of all. In her book, Tina shows how God healed her marriage to Ron and taught both of them to walk in obedience to God's plan for their lives. The book is rich with experience and wisdom for life and will give readers practical guidance.

DR. DAVID KOOP
Pastor, Coastal Church, Vancouver BC

How God Used "the Other Woman"

How God Used "the Other Woman"

Saving Your Marriage after Infidelity

Tina Konkin

TYNDALE HOUSE PUBLISHERS, INC.
CAROL STREAM, ILLINOIS

FOCUS ON THE FAMILY® | **FOCUS ON MARRIAGE**™

This book is dedicated first and foremost to the God of second, third, and many more chances. If it wasn't for God's unfailing grace, I would not be here to tell my story.

Also, to all the first responders deployed in crisis situations, you are the defibrillators who snatch life back from the brink of darkness and give hope to all who have experienced the long, dark tunnel of betrayal.

I want to specifically dedicate this book to my personal first responders. Pastors John and Helen Burns, from the bottom of my heart, a book filled with a million pages and each page filled with a million thank-yous would not cover the amount of gratitude I have in my heart for you both. You took me in when I had nowhere to go that dreaded Sunday afternoon and opened my eyes to the truth: What the enemy meant for evil, God would most certainly use for good. Because of you, thousands of marriages have been touched and, God willing, will continue to be touched through our story.

Contents

Fighting Your Way out of the Nightmare *xi*

PART 1: REVEAL

1. I Choose You *3*
2. Back to the Nightmare *11*
3. Mirror, Mirror on the Wall *23*
4. It's a Not-So-Wonderful Life *35*
5. Spiritual Damage *51*

PART 2: REWRITE

6. It's Time to Rewrite *63*
7. Guarding against a Hard Heart *77*
8. Starting Over *97*
9. Rules of Engagement *113*
10. Moving On *123*
11. Protecting Your Kids *131*

PART 3: RENEW

12. A New Perspective *151*
13. Living above the Line *167*
14. I Get To . . . *179*
15. R3 for Life *187*
16. Heartbreak Hill *193*
17. Let's Put It in Gear *209*
18. Building a Loving Legacy *219*

Acknowledgments *229*
Notes *233*
About the Author *235*

Fighting Your Way out
of the Nightmare

SUNDAY WAS MY FAVORITE DAY. I loved everything about Sundays: the big lunch at Grandma's house, the freedom of playing outside with no adult supervision, and most of all, going to church. I couldn't wait to hear my grandma yell out the window, "C'mon, it's time for church!"

Growing up in a small village in Belgium, my cousin and I would often walk to church on our own. I can still feel the cobblestone street under my shiny dress shoes. My mom made me wear those stupid shoes, and it drove me crazy because I couldn't run as fast as my cousin could. But I didn't care how slippery the shoes were; I'd run anyway.

I wanted to be early and sit in the front row of that little basement Sunday school class. I wanted to see every picture go up on the flannel board. I enjoyed the stories about God's love and how He loved me just the way I was. I can remember so many great stories, but my favorites were always the ones about heaven. The teacher told us that in heaven we wouldn't cry anymore and that no one would laugh at us or hurt us ever again. Those stories made me feel good all over.

As the teachers taught about heaven, they also taught us that there was a hell. I didn't like those stories very much. They were scary. I remember being told that hell was going to be lonely and hot, that there would be no water, and nobody would care how much you cried or how much you hurt.

Even though I was pretty young, I'd already experienced some of those hellish feelings. I felt loneliness and abandonment; I felt that no one cared about me. Even so, the teacher's description of hell and my feelings of abandonment and loneliness didn't come anywhere close to how I felt the day years later when I heard these three simple words: "Yes, it's true."

Those three words confirmed betrayal by my husband and my best friend. I had no idea what pain really felt like until the day I learned their affair was real. Those three words almost destroyed my life. Those words turned my life into absolute agony. The sexual abuse, abandonment, bullying, and loneliness I'd suffered as a child could not compare with what I felt the day I heard those words. I felt as if evil forces were attacking me, and I was doing everything in my power to fight back!

Let's Get out of the Nightmare: The R3 Factor

If you've come face-to-face with betrayal as I did, either as the betrayed or the betrayer (it doesn't matter which), this book is for you. If you try your best to apply what you learn here, with God's hand and His grace upon you, I believe you will find healing just as I did. While portions of this book may feel like a hard-to-digest meal at times, you'll feel full and satisfied once you've finished.

This book will walk you through the story of my husband's betrayal with bone-chilling specificity. We were almost certainly headed for divorce. In fact, some pastors suggested exactly that! Yet because Ron and I applied certain healing principles to our marriage, our marriage not only survived but also thrived. And through our Relationship Lifeline ministry, hundreds of other couples have learned to use the same healing principles that we called the "R3 Factor: Reveal, Rewrite, Renew."

Throughout this book and the exercises in various chapters, you will be encouraged to adopt these powerful principles of healing. I will walk you through each step, showing you what it looks like to *reveal*, *rewrite*, and *renew*. You'll learn that *accountability* and *responsibility* are the keys to successfully applying the R3 Factor. I will also share the adverse effects of not applying these key principles.

Simply put, the R3 Factor principles are:

R1: Reveal the hurts of yesterday.

R2: Rewrite your story today.

R3: Renew tomorrow by making your life better than it ever was before.

The first step is the toughest because you must be willing to reveal the hurts, anger, resentment, and toxic baggage you dragged into your relationship.

Secondly, you'll learn how to rewrite your broken story from a new perspective, from a place of compassion and forgiveness.

Lastly, I'll show you how to renew your life, so that the

days ahead are better than they ever were before. This final step of renewing will give you the power to make your life and relationships better than you could ever have imagined or hoped for.

Do the work. See the results. The R3 Factor is real, and it will work for you as it has for me and hundreds of others.

When I considered writing this book, I had to dig deep into my heart to return to the time when all of this happened—when my husband did the inconceivable and cheated on me with my best friend. I wanted to feel the pain again so I could accurately relay it to you. I tried to think about what resource would have helped me at that time.

Of course, the first answer I came to was . . . nothing! Nothing would have helped. I wanted to curl up and die, and though I didn't die, I did spend many nights curled up, bawling my eyes out. After going a bit deeper, I felt the urging of God and the desire to share my story in all of its personal, ugly details to show you that I may be just like you. I am the hurt, the betrayed, the one who held on to baggage for too long. I am the one who felt that the betrayal wasn't *my* issue.

If you, on the other hand, are the betrayer, I want you to know that this book should bring you hope too. You are not scum. We are all guilty of making bad choices, and, unfortunately, this choice is one of the worst offenses in a marriage. Yet that doesn't mean that grace is only for those who have clean hearts. Far from it! Grace is for anyone who dares to believe that Jesus died for the unworthy and the fallen. Consider Romans 5:20-21 (TLB):

The Ten Commandments were given so that all could see the extent of their failure to obey God's laws. But the more we see our sinfulness, the more we see God's abounding grace forgiving us. Before, sin ruled over all men and brought them to death, but now God's kindness rules instead, giving us right standing with God and resulting in eternal life through Jesus Christ our Lord.

Understand and believe that grace is greater than any sin. So here's my story. If you allow me, I'll be your personal guide to go deeper into (yes, I said deeper into) this mess. I know it sounds counterintuitive, but the only way to get *out* is to go deeper *in*. Then, God willing, you'll come out the other side confident that you, too, can experience a stronger connection with your spouse than you ever imagined possible. My hope is that you'll experience all of the healing and joy that Ron and I found.

PART ONE:
REVEAL

I

I Choose You

I COULDN'T IMAGINE *getting into bed with him again. I had never worn pajamas in our married life. That night, though, they were my protection. We were at his father's house. No one knew what had happened. I didn't have a choice. We had to play the game. It forced us to be together. This is where, in hindsight, I saw God's hand in my greatest grief. Looking back, it was an amazing gift. It was the beginning of my healing. If we had not been forced to be together, I certainly would not have chosen to be.*

He rolled over and leaned his entire body into me. He reached his arm around the vintage floral quilt that covered me and pulled me in close. The blanket felt scratchy; I was glad I'd made him take me to buy pajamas. I could not fathom sleeping uncovered next to him.

His affair made me feel ashamed of myself for the first time in our marriage and, quite possibly, in my lifetime. I had always been comfortable with who I was and especially with my body. I knew I was overweight, but Ron had never held that against me. He'd never mentioned it or even casually suggested I diet or hit the gym. I never shrank back from him when he would come up behind me and wrap his arms around me. He hadn't made my weight an issue, so neither did I. But as I lay beside him that night, the inadequacy of my body was all I could think about.

He was having an affair with my best friend. That's right. My best friend. I knew her intimately. I knew she was in great shape. I knew she must have looked great naked. For the first time in my life, I wanted to cover myself in front of my husband. I felt as damaged as a porcelain china doll hit by a wrecking ball, and the harm was complete and unfixable. Now my husband wanted to be next to me, naked and vulnerable. I wasn't having it.

I needed to be covered, even if it meant buying some cheap pajamas. When he touched me, I was still asleep—mostly. I was in that in-between place where you are aware of every sound and movement around you, when your senses are sufficiently heightened.

I heard his every breath, which was so irregular and shallow—unlike his usual deep and relaxed breathing. I sensed his every move. Those old springs in his parents' bed stabbed into me, letting me know he was there next to me, yet all the while reminding me that I didn't know for how long. In that moment, I wished I knew all of his thoughts. They were what I so desperately wanted to hear. The pit in my stomach grew larger, fell deeper. My skin wasn't sure how to receive his embrace. His touch felt familiar and yet foreign, comforting and painful, all at the same time. How could I want to push him away and want him to hold me closer at the same time?

"I choose you."

It was the loudest whisper I'd ever heard. It was robust and sure. Those three words were clearer and more definitive than any words I'd ever heard. There was no hesitation. No question. No tremor. Only pure assurance. I knew it was true. I knew he chose me, just me, and my entire body sank into his. My skin received him with every nerve ending; with every drop of blood in my veins, I could feel him choosing me, wanting me, loving me.

As we lay in bed, I felt closer to him than ever before. Only twenty-four hours earlier, I'd questioned if I even really knew him. My entire world had come crashing down. Everything had imploded. Three words, "I choose you," were what I needed to hear, and I had to believe he meant them. The thing I feared most was that he would try, under pressure and fear of the unknown, to make our marriage work when all along his heart belonged to someone else, and I would experience his resentment. But if he really chose me, I reasoned, then we had a chance to rebuild.

That was the first day of the rest of our lives.

———— •• ————

The Moment of Truth

The truth is, this story didn't start with "I choose you." Before I heard Ron whisper those words, I thought my marriage was over. How could it not be? I couldn't in that moment imagine anything that Ron could do or say to change what he did to me . . . and with my best friend!

I'll never forget the day I received the phone call that changed the course of my marriage. It was January 5, 1998, and I was standing in my home office, surrounded by cards from the man I loved and photos of beautiful times in our seventeen years together. But that day was not like any other day. On that day it was brought to my attention that my husband—my life partner, the father of my children, and my best friend in the world—had cheated on me and was having an actual affair.

Someone had suggested that Ron was having an affair, and that day, over the phone, was the day that I had to ask him that dreaded question.

"Is it true? Is it? Tell me it's not true."

"Yes, it's true."

With these three words, life as I knew it was over.

"With her?"

"Yes. With her."

"My best friend?"

"Yes, it's true . . ." His voice dropped.

My heart sank, and I prayed I was in a nightmare. I prayed this was just a disgusting dream. I prayed that I could erase this day forever. I had to sit down.

I had experienced horrible dreams before during those PMS times when hormones go crazy. I would dream that Ron was leaving me or had died, but then I would roll over and wake him up. He was always so good. He would wake up every time and comfort me. He would hold me tight and whisper gently in my ear that he was right there and going nowhere. Oh, how I prayed that this was just another one of those PMS dreams. But no, this time I was wide-awake and it was all very real.

The doorbell rang, and I had to snap back to another reality.

"I have to go."

"What?"

"I have to go, Ron."

A Divine Distraction

I hung up the phone, not out of anger or any other emotion, but because the doorbell was ringing. My thoughts became matter-of-fact. *Answer the door.* That's what you do when someone is at the door. You answer it. I just had to answer the door. One foot in front of the other, I began to walk toward it.

Suddenly, as I stood at the top of the stairs facing the door with my hand outstretched to open it, I felt God stop me. I heard that still, small voice inside say: *Don't open* that *door—the door to divorce. If he walks out that door, let it not be because you opened it for him. That will be on him. He will make the decision to stay or go. It will not be because you kicked him out.*

Everything in me was screaming bloody murder. I was sure Ron wouldn't need to walk out the door—I'd be waiting with a gun! He didn't have to worry about me divorcing him; he had to worry about the vow I had made that only death would separate us . . .

I shook my head, trying to clear that image from my mind. At that moment, I was in no place to hear from God.

The doorbell rang again. Previously I had advertised my car for sale and agreed to show it, but that was before I knew my life was falling apart.

That was before the instant I had learned my entire world was crashing down.

I opened the door. The poor guy—he had no clue what he was dealing with. The man had the friendliest disposition, and he immediately started in with small talk. I wanted to yell at him for being happy. He thought it was important to tell me that, though his drive had taken more than an hour, "It was a beautiful day, and the rain had stopped." *Did he think I really cared?*

His sixteen-year-old daughter looked even happier. It was a father-daughter date, and he was buying her a car. *Father-daughter date.* I knew all about those; after all, Ron had prided himself on being a *great* father. I wondered what his daughter would think of her "perfect" dad now! My head was still pounding from the words "Yes, it's true," but I managed to hand the man the keys so he could test-drive the car.

I was in a slow-motion sequence—the minutes ticked away like hours. Finally, the man and his daughter returned from the test drive, and he started walking around the car. We stood in the driveway. It took him forever to make a decision. My "inside" voice was so loud, I thought he surely could hear me saying: *Quit hemming and hawing. Do you want to buy the car or not? It's a car. Just a stupid car. It's gold and has four doors and four wheels, and it drives. It will never cheat on you or hurt you or make you feel like your whole life is a lie. It's a car. Do you want it or not? Forget it. Forget it; it's not for sale. Forget the whole thing. If you can't make one stupid little decision like buying a stupid car, then I don't want you to have it anyway.*

"I'll take it," the man said.

"Great. It's a good little car. I think your daughter will like it."

Looking back, I know that this man didn't just haphazardly ring my doorbell. In fact, I know that it was a divine appointment, a *divine distraction*. I added this story of selling a car during a crisis to highlight the following lesson.

Watch for God

It was just a black rubber bracelet worth maybe fifty cents, the kind kids receive at Bible camp. It was worthless, but the message it bore remained priceless: *Watch for God.* That bracelet reminded the wearer that, even in the mundane, ordinary things of our lives, God speaks . . . if we will only tune in to hear Him. I remembered that bracelet and the lesson it contained for years.

Watch for God. I want you to write these three words somewhere you will see them often, preferably several times a day. Write them on a sticky note and put it on your refrigerator door, on your bathroom mirror, on the wall behind your sink.

The simplicity of answering that door changed my mind-set and how I subsequently reacted to my husband. If I had stayed on the phone another minute, our conversation wouldn't have ended well. God knew my toxic thoughts needed an interruption, and He used a simple doorbell to break the shock of what I was hearing. It was almost like when a hypnotist snaps his fingers, and the people who seconds before were under his "spell" immediately snap back to reality. In this case the doorbell snapped me out of the drama and trauma and into the mundane. It was exactly what needed to happen. God will use anything and everything to our advantage, as it says in Romans 8:28: "And we know that for those who love God all things work together for good, for those who are called according to his purpose."

I've included this story so you can understand how God orchestrates every part of our lives. Every appointment can be divine if you are only open to seeing it that way. God will use what we allow Him to use, and He will intervene because He loves us in spite of the mess we find ourselves in or the mess we make. For me, answering the doorbell that day was a divine intervention. After this, watching for God became a way of life for me, and I know it can become a way of life for you as well!

2

Back to the Nightmare

FINALLY, I WAS ABLE *to call Ron. He had left early that morning and driven to his parents' home to visit his dad. He was eight hours away from home—our home. The home we built together with our two kids. The home where we made memories and plans. The home where we made love. At that moment, my heart believed we might never share this home again.*

Ron had a good reason to visit his dad. His mom had just passed away of cancer the week before, and Ron wanted to be with his father. Thinking back, I'm sure he also needed some time away to sort himself out.

As I dialed Ron's number my brain went into a kind of shock. Suddenly, everything became clear. One might think that with this heartbreaking news, my mind would be foggy or moving in slow motion, but it wasn't. I could see everything, hear everything, feel everything.

And I had questions about everything.

How? How did this happen? How could you? How did I not know?

When? When did this start? When did it happen? When were you lying and when were you telling the truth?

Where? Where did it happen? Where were you? Where was she? Where was I?

And then the dreaded why . . . Why? Why? Why? Why would you do this to me? Why would you do this to our kids? Why would you destroy our family? What were you thinking?

I remember the day about eight months earlier when Ron had walked out of his office, having just counseled a man who had cheated on his wife. They had five children. Ron shook his head as that session ended.

"I'll never understand what goes through a man's head, how he can believe that he won't get caught or that he'll get away with this," he told me. Ron said he'd called the man an idiot, adding, "I hope your thirty-second thrill of being with another woman was worth all you are about to lose, buddy."

I remember saying, "That's not what you said, I hope."

"You bet that's what I said."

I couldn't believe Ron could be so blunt, but the man kept coming back as we tried to help him and his wife restore what was left of their marriage.

Now the tables had been turned. This was my husband who had cheated on me, and now I wanted to call him the idiot.

The questions kept coming: Why don't you love me? Why did you do this? Why wasn't I enough? Why did you want her? Why? Why? Why?

I stood in my small home office, tears streaming down my

face, confusion in my heart. My mind was trying to figure out how this could be true. Old greeting cards surrounded me. I had displayed these precious cards as trophies because they represented Ron's love for me. They all had the same theme. They were black-and-white pictures of a little boy and girl dancing together, a little boy and girl holding hands, a little boy giving a little girl a red rose. He knew how much I loved those cards.

Ron answered the phone after three short rings, but it seemed like an eternity as my mind raced through the litany of questions I wanted answers to . . . and some I'd probably rather not know the answers to.

I was looking at those cards, and I could barely breathe. "This has all been a lie."

"No. No, it hasn't. It's not. It's not a lie."

"The cards you wrote me have all been lies. Every one of them."

"Tina, no, that's not true. I meant every word."

But I couldn't hear that. I hung up the phone. Everything had changed. And it had happened in my office, the same office where, ironically, numerous other women had asked for help. It was in this same room that I had comforted them and counseled them through what I was now facing. Countless women and couples had sat on that same small mauve love seat and listened, many times while wiping tears from their eyes, as I convinced them that there is always hope.

"God is bigger than this pain, and He is our healer," I would tell them, and that was something I believed wholeheartedly. Every time, without fail, no matter what their story sounded like or how much pain they were currently experiencing, I would boldly instill faith in them individually and collectively. My goal was to make sure that, before they left my office, they would have *hope renewed and directed toward a loving God, whose promises and love cover a multitude of sins.*

It was surreal. It was the dreaded nightmare. This couldn't be happening to us! We are relationship counselors. We heal families. We heal the brokenhearted. Now I was brokenhearted. It didn't make sense. Who was going to sit me on that healing love seat and renew my hope? Convince me to have faith in my spouse? Give me peace?

The call had ended. Now what? It was early Sunday afternoon. The kids were away, I'd sold a car, and as I stood in my brightly lit house, I saw only darkness. A dark cloud had descended on that house, and at that moment, I would've welcomed death.

Ironically, the house had been built in the 1960s when people were afraid of the Cold War. It had been constructed with a bunker, which we used for storage. The bunker was dark and damp, but it was meant to be a safe hiding place, safe from nuclear warfare. I wished there had been some sort of a bunker for my heart, something to shield me from this explosion. But there wasn't. I never even saw it coming.

The Trance

I decided to call our pastors and ask if I could see them. I couldn't be alone; I needed help. As I entered their home I felt numb. I shared the story with them, and they were shocked, to say the least. They had known Ron for years; this was not the man they knew. These were the pastors who had trusted us with other hurting couples and individuals, yet now we were like the shoemaker with holes in his shoes. As they sat there, all they could do to encourage me was pray and tell me not to make any quick decisions.

Shortly after prayer, our pastor's wife said: "Tina, I believe Ron is in a trance. You need to go to him." (I still thank God for her advice that afternoon.) She continued: "You need to go to him and see him face-to-face. This trance needs to be broken, and he needs to face reality."

Let me tell you, there is no price for wise counsel. The hour I spent with our pastors, and the subsequent thirty-second revelation I received, changed what could have been a sure end to our marriage. Hearing that woman tell me that my husband was in a trance and not in his right mind changed everything for me. If Ron and I had stayed apart for days, I believe doing so would have allowed the enemy to kill our fragile, troubled marriage.

Let's talk about that trance. Often with infidelity comes a rush of excitement, an infusion of "new." There is a trance of deception that becomes the new reality for people caught up in this sin. People fall into the trap of believing these heat-of-the-moment emotions, a flame fanned by the stroking of the ego and the fulfillment of unmet desires. But this flame has been lit with mere paper or small kindling. It will almost never continue to burn because it has no real fuel source. It's important to understand that this state of false euphoria is the trance; this is not generally the true desire of the adulterer.

The trance reminds me of those commercials about a seemingly magic pill where everything sounds great and wonderful—until the end, when all of the side effects are listed. They are usually a million times worse than the original problem could ever be. Usually, the person in the trance is going after only the good feelings without regard to the consequences of his or her actions. It's like smokers not seeing health warnings on the back side of a cigarette pack because they're blinded by addiction. No one wants to hear about the side effects, only the good feelings. This is the trance in a nutshell.

As I considered the suggestion of seeing Ron face-to-face, I thought of the biggest question I had: "What were you thinking?" When something terrible happens, why are we inclined to ask that particular question? Isn't the answer obvious? In retrospect, that might have been the dumbest question I could have asked. Even still, I asked it, and you might have as well.

Months before all of this drama took place, my niece got into trouble at school. The school called me since they weren't able to reach my sister, and I left my home office thinking, *That girl is lucky they couldn't reach her mom right now!* I'd always had a soft spot in my heart for that particular niece. I began making excuses for her behavior. *It was probably peer pressure*, I thought. *Go easy on her.*

Of course, the moment my niece stepped into the van, I forgot all of my own counsel. Before she could even fasten her seat belt, I yelled out her name and asked that dumb question, "What were you thinking?" Without missing a beat, she replied, "That's the problem, Auntie Tina! I *wasn't* thinking."

You can probably see where this is going. When people do things outside of their character, chances are they are not thinking at all.

My Call for Help

As I left my pastors' home that evening, my heart felt some relief, but my mind was still spinning out of control. I knew I could not simply hop on a flight and show up. I needed to call Ron and ask him if I could come. I started to feel those old roots of rejection come up: *What if he says no?* But I had to make the call; I had to lay my fear of rejection aside and listen to my pastor's wise counsel.

I dialed that old familiar number . . . it rang once, and then it rang again. I could feel a lump rising in my throat . . . it rang a third time. This time, Ron answered. His voice was somber; I could barely hear him. I knew the reality of his dark secret had hit him, too. For a moment, there was silence. It was as if we no longer knew each other. It felt so awkward.

Finally, I broke the silence. "Can I come and see you?" There was silence again, and my heart sank. If he said no, I didn't have a plan B. The lump in my throat was now the size of a grapefruit.

The silence broke. "I can't stop you if you want to come."

That's not what I wanted to hear.

I wanted him to *want* to be with me.

I wanted to hear, "Of course. Please come. I need to be with you."

It hurt.

I responded, "I really want your blessing in coming."

Ron's voice became husky, and I knew he was crying. "Why would you even want to see me right now? The last person you should want to be with is me."

I didn't answer his question; I knew in my heart that if my

pastor was right, then I needed to see him. I needed to pray that the trance would break.

Softly, he said, "If you want to come, then come."

Loving Two Women at One Time

Ron was filled with anxiety; this much I knew. I could hear it in his voice when we talked on the phone. I was scheduled to arrive in Trail, British Columbia, the next morning, and his family had no idea what we were going through. That night, as he tried to go to bed, all Ron could do was toss and turn, consumed by the guilt of what he had done. He had to talk to someone. Sitting up in bed, he grabbed the phone. He decided to call his sister Donna, who lived next door to their father's farm.

"I need to talk to you, Donna. I'm in trouble. Can I come over?" He could hear his sister immediately sit up in her bed.

Donna, in her bustling, perpetually interested fashion (especially when it came to her little brother), replied, "Of course, Ronnie. I'll put the kettle on."

Ron drove up the hill to the top of her property. As he walked into that log home, filled with so many happy memories of our kids playing together, of big Christmas dinners, of our ski trips, he suddenly felt a darkness about the place. Ron knew he was about to confess something that his sister would not like. After all, he was the "golden child." He had never rebelled. He had seemingly been the perfect husband, and definitely the perfect dad. And after all, he was in the ministry.

In spite of all this, Ron knew he needed to tell her before

I arrived. It was close to 11 p.m. when he got to her house, and they sat in front of her large, warm fireplace with tea in hand. As he told her what had transpired, Ron could see the shock on his sister's face, and she didn't hold back from berating him with one question after the other, telling him she couldn't believe it.

"How could this happen?" Donna asked. "How could this happen to you and Tina? Did you lose your mind? Did you have a temporary moment of insanity?"

Here were the very questions he himself had asked other men who were willing to throw everything away because they had succumbed to temptation and the thrill of the moment.

Donna continued the tirade: "How could you do this to Tina? You guys always seemed like the most loving couple!" Shaking her head sadly, she added, "Ron, you teach *other* people how to do life together!"

"I Never Stopped Loving You . . ."

His sister's words were piercing, and Ron kept saying, "I don't know, I don't know."

And then Donna asked the big question: "When did you stop loving Tina?"

Immediately he responded, "I never did; I never stopped loving her." He felt sick as he looked up and asked Donna, "How do you love two women at the same time?" Shaking his head, Ron continued, "You have no idea how confused I am."

His sister listened, trying to absorb everything her little brother was telling her, yet it all amounted to this one conclusion: He was not the man everyone thought him to be, including her. I'm sure Donna wondered how Ron could hide such a secret. I'm also sure she knew it was tearing him apart inside. So his sister patiently listened as Ron continued pouring his heart out to her, telling her how terrible the past year had been.

"Tina is oblivious as to why we have drifted so far apart. It's as if she's in her own world, a world I can't find a place in, or maybe don't have a place in. I feel like I gave up trying to make her happy somewhere along the line. Work seems to be the only thing that she really enjoys, the only thing that has her heart. That's what keeps her happy, and it appears to be the only thing she's interested in.

"Thank God we work together, or I would've lost any connection to her a long time ago. I know I sound like I'm making excuses, but honestly, I've never asked for much, and this year with Mom dying, Tina's even more distant from me than she has ever been. That's what started this whole connection with the other woman. This other woman *cared* about what I was going through. She saw that I was in pain. She reached out to comfort me."

Imagine your flesh and blood, someone you looked up to and admired, someone you knew intimately, sitting in front of you broken and crying, telling you his deepest, darkest failures. His sister was simply heartbroken at his admission: "I wish I could stay, or I wish I could leave, but both have my heart. I honestly feel sick. And now," he added, "Tina is coming tomorrow morning." Donna didn't know what to say.

I don't know much else about what happened that night, except that my sister-in-law called me afterward as I lay in bed, crying. It was past midnight when I answered the phone. Donna's voice was a comfort to me because I knew she loved me.

"Tina," she said, "I don't know what to say to you right now, but I believe Ron has not stopped loving you. He's very confused right now. Trust me, I nearly beat him with a wooden spoon. I could have choked him!"

For some reason, those words were comforting to me, but then she said: "I saw my little brother Ronnie, and I knew that this was not him. Tina, I'm praying. I know right now it doesn't feel this way, but I know that God will do a miracle here."

"Donna, do you believe Ron's in a trance right now?"

I could hear her sad but hopeful laugh. "Ron's definitely out there somewhere. It's crazy how he let this happen. There's no making sense of it. Let's talk some more tomorrow."

I hung up the phone and tried to sleep. It was strange, but in a funny sort of way I couldn't help but feel comforted by the conversation. Suddenly, I knew I wasn't alone, and I truly believed that God had provided me with another person who wanted to see our marriage restored almost as much as I did.

Even so, I couldn't help but feel like Humpty Dumpty, except it seemed like my great fall would last forever. My life felt like one of those dreams where you fall into a never-ending abyss of pure darkness. There was no end in sight, and I wasn't landing anywhere. I felt as if I were disappearing deeper and deeper into a cold, empty pit.

In my family, I'm the one who doesn't like heights. I never thought jumping off cliffs or bungee jumping was something I needed to experience. So, of course, it would stand to reason that I'd now find myself falling endlessly off a cliff into the unknown with no water to land in or even a harness and rope to help support me or save me. All these thoughts were running through my mind as I lay in the darkness. Eventually I fell asleep from sheer physical and emotional exhaustion, with one last thought playing itself over and over: If this is a trance, then it can be broken!

Sometimes all a person needs is a little bit of hope—a statement, a gesture, even a word—to release you from your free fall, to allow you to see that the world hasn't gone completely dark. There is still a slight ray of light, way off in the distance, if you look hard enough. That ray of light for me was hearing Ron's sister tell me that he had never stopped loving me. I latched on to that sentence like my life depended on it, and to some degree, it did.

If you think hard, might you be able to find a tiny ray of hope for yourself right now? Don't overthink it. Don't force it or fight it. Just reflect and silently still your heart and see if you can't hear something differently or see or remember something in a new context. Words and actions can change depending on the state of our own hearts and especially our hurts. Step aside from the hurt and try to find your ray of hope.

3

Mirror, Mirror on the Wall

I DON'T REMEMBER *falling asleep that night, but I do remember how I felt at six o'clock the next morning when the alarm went off. I have never been drunk, but I have heard many people say that the "morning after" is the worst. I remember thinking, If* this is what the morning after feels like, then I never want to be here again. *I felt like I had ridden an emotional roller coaster all night long.*

Have you ever looked into the mirror while you were crying? After crying the "ugly cry," the cry that has taken on a life of its own, causing you to lose all control? The cry itself is now in control of you. You can barely catch your breath between sobs, and you start to lose strength and stamina. You feel like a kid who has forgotten what she is crying about but keeps crying anyway. You might be walking around aimlessly when you catch a glimpse of yourself in the mirror and suddenly wonder, Do I actually look like this when I'm crying?

After having one of those cries all night, it seemed, I woke up not sure if I'd slept at all. I remembered tossing and turning, more awake than asleep, trying to figure out what was real. Wanting to understand, I envisioned a puzzle on my bed that I was trying to put together. The sheets and blanket were all a mess, and I couldn't get the pieces to fit. To top it off, I didn't have a flat surface, so nothing could stick together. Suddenly, in that mysterious, dreamlike way, all of the pieces came together, and there across my entire bed was an image of the two of them, Ron and my best friend. The puzzle was complete, and staring back at me were their smiling faces. The puzzle had come to life, and they were looking right at me, coldly shrugging their shoulders and apologizing, yet with no remorse. I gasped for air and woke up from this nightmare. I don't know how long it took me to drift back to sleep again.

As I opened my eyes the next morning, my mind was foggy—everything was hazy and surreal. I threw the blankets back, got up, and made my way to the bathroom. The tile countertop of our 1960s house was cold and speckled; the sink was pink and stained with water. In autopilot, I brushed my teeth and rinsed my face, carefully wiping any water off the edge of the counter, as was my habit, because Ron hated when he leaned over and his shirt and pants would get wet.

Ron. Ron wasn't here. Right. Abruptly, the autopilot was jolted off, and I was awake. The bathroom mirror was a wall-to-wall medicine cabinet, and as I glanced up to dry my face, checking to see if I looked as terrible as I felt, my swollen, bloodshot eyes peered deep into my broken heart, and I said out loud, "God, why? How could he do this to me? How could she do this to me?" I continued my tirade, "God, how could You let this happen?"

As clear as day, I heard God say, with the reflection of my sad face looking back at me, "What role did you play in this, Tina?"

My heart stopped. "I'm sorry, what did You say?" I gave my head a shake, but God said it again: "What role did you play in this?"

"Are you kidding me? I'm the victim here. He cheated. Not me. This was done to me. This has got to be a joke. This can't be God saying this!"

It took me a minute, but I knew His voice well. Oh yes, it was God, and He was challenging me to reason past the pain. This was the moment my life changed—a moment I would never forget.

———— • ————

Facing the Woman in the Mirror

In the moment of my deepest devastation, after learning my husband was having an affair with my best friend, I had to face this question with swollen eyes and a shredded heart:

Tina, what role did you play in this?

You would think that God would give me a break! After all, it hadn't even been twenty-four hours since I'd received the worst news of my life. But I thank God that His timing is always perfect, that He doesn't bother to adjust His plan to suit our schedule. I'm also thankful that His thoughts are higher than ours; after all, He does have a better vantage point and always sees the big picture.

Being able to see the entire story definitely has its advantages. God knew I needed to face myself before I faced my husband of sixteen years. I had approximately two hours before I arrived in Ron's hometown. God had only two hours to get me to where I needed to be: completely transparent and vulnerable. I needed to be like an open wound, ready to receive the stinging but healing antiseptic salve.

As I stood in front of that mirror, my reflection gazing back at me, I heard God's voice loud and clear. I knew I had a choice to make. I could choose to stay in a "victim mode," blaming everything on my husband and the "other woman," or I could decide to shed the victim cloak and start exploring my part in this mess. Victims don't heal; they usually spend their lives blaming everything and everyone. I totally understand this; it's easier to blame others than to look inside ourselves. Furthermore, blaming someone else and remaining in the victim mode makes it impossible to heal.

It was time for me to look at all the negative stuff I'd dragged into my marriage. I have to admit, though, that the question God was asking me was so difficult that I had to brace myself for what I would see. The thought that I had, in any way, participated in the affair or the degradation of my own marriage was like an emotional foreign invader. Holding this question in my mind elicited a nauseous gut reaction. It was almost too much to take. But one of the principles I had learned in working with hundreds of people on a very personal level was that the way out of this mess wouldn't include blaming my husband or friend. Though I didn't understand exactly how, I knew that healing my destroyed life would include a counterintuitive approach. Though I wasn't directly involved in the act that almost ruined my marriage, I also knew that I wouldn't have the luxury of standing on the sidelines. I knew I would have to join this mess and ask myself the most difficult question imaginable:

What role did I play in this?

How did I knowingly or unknowingly play a part in the drama unfolding before me? I had to trust in God and His infinite wisdom and be willing to embark on the journey, fully committed. I had to trust that if God asked the question, He already knew the answer. It was time to "put up or shut up."

I decided to submit to God and face what would come next, knowing that whatever it was, my God would protect me, guide me, and carry me, even when I crumbled under the weight of this next chapter of my life. I knew it wouldn't be easy, but I also knew my Bible was His sovereign Word, something I could depend on without hesitation. And to some extent, my entire life *did* depend on it. I had to believe Philippians 1:6: "I am sure of this, that he who began a good work in you will bring it to completion at the day of Jesus Christ."

If you are willing to face the question, "What part did I play?" you will be able to start your journey toward healthy thinking, which is necessary to produce healthy decisions. Choices made out of pain are not healthy, and these unhealthy decisions affect not only you but also (if applicable) your children.

My own personal "mirror experience" hasn't always been received well by betrayed spouses, and understandably so. I remember one young woman who, in front of her entire

Relationship Lifeline group, had a visibly disagreeable reaction when I shared my story of accountability.

"Awwwwww," she remarked sarcastically.

The attention of the entire class immediately shifted from me, the speaker, to the young woman who had uttered this remark. I noticed that her body posture made her intention unmistakably clear. She was not happy about what I was saying, and she was not at all afraid to express her displeasure.

Needless to say, the class was suddenly pin-drop quiet as everyone waited to see my reaction. I slowly moved toward this young woman, intentionally getting up close and personal. The chairs in our workshops are set up in a U shape, and she was in the center. Perfect. Standing in front of her, I asked, "Is there something I said that has offended you?" She was quick to answer, as though she expected me to confront her.

"Yes, as a matter of fact! If you think for one minute that I'm going to take responsibility for what this man—" she said as she pointed to her husband— "has done to our family and me, I've got news for you *and* him! He took his pants down all by himself. He's a big boy, and I did not help him do that. So I am the victim here!"

I needed to let her have her moment, and let me tell you, she sure did! I know what those intense emotions feel like, so I let her finish her rant, but I also knew I couldn't leave her in that emotional space. Therefore, while I acknowledged that she was right—she should never take responsibility for her husband's indiscretion because his decision to be with another woman was totally his and his alone—I had to give her some food for thought. "Can I ask you a question?" I asked.

"Sure," she replied.

"Would you say that your marriage, even before the affair, was not perfect?"

"Yes," she quickly answered.

Encouraged by her response, I proceeded to ask my second question: "Do you think you could maybe own 10 percent of why it was not as good as it could have been?"

Everyone in the group could see her demeanor change. Her body relaxed. She sighed, and her reply was soft and quiet. "Yes, honestly, even more than 10 percent." With that simple admission, the tide had turned for this young lady.

Compassionately, I responded, "Then just own 100 percent of whatever you're responsible for."

Truth Is Your Friend

When you walk into the meeting room at our Relationship Lifeline weekend workshops, the first thing you see is a small banner saying "Tell the Truth." On day one it is hardly noticeable, as it is set up intentionally to not stand out. But as the days unfold, the sign grows larger and seems to demand more attention. The only path to growth and healing is for you to be honest with yourself, to reveal what events in your past have led you to this point in your life. You must make the decision that *truth* is your friend.

Truth is the guide you need to find your way back to health. Truth is everything. Make truth your best friend. If you let God open your eyes, He will show you all that lies hidden in the depth of your heart, all that you've spent years trying to hide because of embarrassment or shame. He will even show you your hidden self, and then He will heal you. That's the good news! He won't peel your heart open like an onion and leave you there. He will gently open up your wounds, apply salve to them, and then heal what you once considered unmendable. He is God. He is love. He *can* and *will* heal you, but you have to be open, honest, and fully committed to the process. You have to seek truth alongside Him.

If you are feeling anything like I was as I looked into that mirror, you are terrified right now. But can I tell you this: If you fight through your fears, even as scary as this is, God will walk with you. Please don't let anything, especially the enemy, whose stated mission is to kill, steal, and destroy, rob you of the healing God has promised. God's desire is to see you fully recover from this hurt. He wants to take you by the hand and travel the road to recovery and restoration with you. Don't pass up this offer, and don't think about the marriage right now. This healing is for *you* and about *you*. Focus on getting healthy and dropping the baggage of hurt, anger, insecurity, abandonment, loss, and whatever else has been hiding in your heart. Focus on healing *you*!

The Real Enemy

If you believe in God, then like it or not, you also believe there is a devil. Think about what the enemy has tried to steal, kill, and destroy in you, even before your marriage existed. What lies does he have you convinced are truths? What truths does he have you convinced are lies? Is the enemy controlling your thought life, especially right now? Or should I ask, is he still controlling you and running you ragged?

One of the things I've learned from the many years I've been blessed with life and ministry is that the devil is a lot of things, all of them horrible and nasty, but the one thing he is *not* is impatient. He will wait you out. He will sit back and watch you struggle and contemplate and debate, and then when you are at your most vulnerable, like a lion waiting for his prey to get distracted, he will pounce.

The apostle Peter describes it like this in 1 Peter 5:8: "Be sober-minded; be watchful. Your adversary the devil prowls around like a roaring lion, seeking someone to devour."

Right now, my friend, it is vital that you keep a sober, rational, sound mind, even if the last thing you're feeling is sober and rational. Making decisions now from a closed-off, hurting heart that can only see the devastation and feel the hurt could negatively affect the rest of your life and your family's life in ways you can't even consider at this moment.

So no matter what else you do right now, I'm asking you to *stop*. Let God take this one! Your task is to actively resist the devil as he tries to convince you that you're a victim, that you get a free pass to act as your emotions drive you. You are not a *victim*, so don't fall into that trap. And trust me, it *is* a trap, one the devil has set just for you while he waits for you to walk right into it. Instead, let me remind you of 1 John 4:4: "Little children, you are from God and have overcome them, for he who is in you is greater than he who is in the world."

Take charge of your own life and own your baggage, make truth your best friend, and trust that God is walking with you through it all. It's time to change your perspective *and* your life. Start looking at the power you have—the power of the Creator of the universe who promises to walk with you every step of the way, no matter what.

With that promise firmly in place, doesn't it seem silly to fight this with your own strength? Let God steer. He is so much better at it than you, or me, or anyone else ever will be. Resist the devil, as it says in 1 Peter 5:9: "Resist him, firm in your faith, knowing that the same kinds of suffering are being experienced by your brotherhood throughout the world."

My prayer for you is that you understand and believe in your heart that you are not alone. Let this story of my suffering, my healing, and the restoration of my marriage, followed by the greatest days of both my life and Ron's, give you hope. Countless others have been healed and restored; they have gone on to have incredible, wonderful marriages that they once would have never believed possible. Don't give up, and don't give in to the lies of the devil.

A Word to the Betrayer

You might think that I'm only going to address the betrayed spouses in this book; let me assure you, that's not the case. This book applies to all involved equally: the betrayed, the betrayer, or the other man or woman. The Bible says it best in Romans 3:23: "For all have sinned and fall short of the glory of God."

We all have a part to play in the drama resulting from adult choices. This book speaks to those choices and tries to address a pathway to healing and a better life despite past decisions. Every word in this book is meant for *all* of us, no matter the "side" we find ourselves on. Nothing changes the fact that our enemy prowls around all of us like a starving lion waiting to destroy his prey by filling them with shame and guilt. Yes, if you are the "other" man (or woman), you have sinned and there are consequences you'll undoubtedly have to pay. The pain you have caused your family, and whoever else may have been hurt by your actions, is very real, but never doubt for even a second that God will forgive you and renew your life. He is faithful to fulfill His promises to His people.

The key is to do the right thing right now and repent. Repent from the heart for your hurtful actions, seek forgiveness from those you've hurt, and then forgive yourself.

If you walk around wearing a cloak of unforgiveness, a cape of shame, and a mantle of guilt, then you are most certainly not walking in God's will. To continue walking like this suggests you are willing to nullify Christ's torturous death on the cross and the absolute power of His resurrection. Don't fall prey to the enemy's suggestion that you, a mere human being, can cancel out the reason Jesus died for you.

You may have heard this for years, maybe even decades, but let me remind you that Jesus died for *you*. Yes, *you* personally, because He loves *you*. Don't lose that message in the vastness of the "Jesus died for the entire world" truth. Bring that statement home. Bring it into your heart, and own it. Personalize it—Jesus died for you so you might live life more abundantly. Settle it in your heart that His plan for your life is a good one, a plan not to harm you but to give you hope (see Jeremiah 29:11).

When you personalize that truth, you'll realize what it actually means: "Jesus died for *my* sin. He did it so that *I* could be called blameless." So whether you are the betrayed or the betrayer, take heart in knowing that Jesus died for you both equally! As 1 John 1:8-9 tells us, not one of us is blameless: "If we say we have no sin, we deceive ourselves, and the truth is not in us. If we confess our sins, he is faithful and just to forgive us our sins and to cleanse us from all unrighteousness."

The Bible is clear on the steps you need to take, no matter your role in the situation. Let none of us claim to be without sin. No one has the right to throw a stone, just as no one deserves to be stoned.

4

It's a Not-So-Wonderful Life

I CLOSED MY EYES and took a deep breath. Okay, God, let's do this, *I prayed.* Help me to see what role I played in all of this. I'm willing to take an honest look at myself—my baggage and my damage, which I thought I was well aware of. Right now, I really want to feel sorry for myself. I want to be the victim. I want to use my right as "the betrayed." God, I know You're trying to show me that I need to take responsibility. For this marriage to work, for us to have a chance at restoring our marriage, for me to be free, I know I need to do this. I know I can't control or take responsibility for anybody else's actions, but I can look at mine. I do have control over how I react and respond to this. And I know You will lead me. So show me, God, what role did I play in all of this?

Even as I said the words—and though everything in me knew I had to do what was right—oh, how I wanted to do what was so wrong! I wanted to blame Ron, blame my friend, and ultimately blame God. I could relate to the apostle Paul at that moment, knowing I should do what was right but still wanting to do what was wrong (see Romans 7:15).

As soon as I made the decision to be willing to see my part in this situation, I recalled a vivid, painful memory. I saw myself in a funeral home, twenty-one years old, standing over the dead body of the man I had loved—my former boyfriend who had battled cancer at the age of twenty-five and passed away far too soon. I was having my final moments with him, saying good-bye, and placing a red rose on his chest. In this vision, the red rose stood out because it was alive.

How could it still be alive after all these years?

God, what does this have to do with anything? I haven't thought about this in years.

My heart started to race. The Lord was silent.

Continuing to observe the scene unfolding before me, I watched myself as I placed that rose on his chest. It was then my eyes were opened, and the Lord showed me that the red rose represented my heart. My heart had made a vow that I would never love or nurture another man the way I had cared for this boyfriend throughout his battle with cancer. I locked up a piece of my heart the day he died because the pain was too much to bear, and I vowed to never give it to anybody again. With the closing of that coffin that day, I had closed my heart. I cried out to God, "Please forgive me."

My spirit sank as I realized I had been withholding my heart from my husband. My partner. My love. The one who had given me everything. The one who had vowed to love me forever. He had not received that love in return in all those years—not in full, anyway. Instead, the love I gave Ron was guarded and fearful. I had withheld my real love from him.

Right then, I remembered all of the times I had rejected Ron. I saw every time he'd reached out to nurture me and I was cold toward him. I saw the times when he needed a word of encouragement and I was silent, the times when he needed me to hold his hand and I clenched my fist, the times when he desired for me to make the first move but I refused to budge from my position. I saw the days when he was discouraged, yet I offered no comfort. I saw the cup of coffee I didn't bring, the shoulder rub I didn't give, the nurture I had locked away and buried. My heart had been hard and cold.

Oh, the "hardness of heart" that Jesus had spoken of to the Pharisees about divorce in Matthew 19:8—there it was! I saw it! Nevertheless, in that moment of revelation, I'm not sure if I felt relief or sorrow.

I cried out, "God, I didn't realize what I was doing!"

Then I remembered Jesus' words on the cross: "Father, forgive them, for they know not what they do." That was me! Little by little, I had been pushing Ron away without knowing what I was doing. I pushed him away because of my pain, because of my unresolved issues, because of my hurt, my fear, and my wounds.

God, forgive me. I did play a role in this. How do I heal? How do I change?

I knew at that point that I had to take a step back and

review my life, because sometimes you need to have an honest discussion about your past to move on to the future.

Where Did It All Go Wrong?

It was 1997, and it had been our best year yet. Our marriage was strong, and our business, Relationship Lifeline, was in its second year and flourishing. We saw more marriages and more individuals healed than ever before. Our difficult years, it seemed, were over.

Before Relationship Lifeline started, I had lived through five arduous years filled with what seemed like constant defeat: from my eighty-pound weight gain in eight months to feeling like the worst wife and mom, especially to my eight-year-old daughter, to a full-blown depression.

Thankfully, by the summer of 1997, Ron and I were finally in a place where everything was better than I could remember it ever being. I remember looking at Ron one day when we were on a drive and saying, "I am so thankful that you're my man." He turned to look at me and said, "You've never made me feel better as a husband and as a man than you did just now." It was an incredible year.

Yet that same year Ron's mom was diagnosed with pancreatic cancer. It was a shock to all of us, as she had been healthy and had taken excellent care of herself.

Ron took the news hard, and I could see him retreating into a secluded area of his heart so deep I couldn't reach him. He became increasingly quiet—so quiet that I knew he was withdrawing from the children and me.

He did everything he could, made every excuse to avoid

all social events: suppertime, family time, church—even Christmas, which had always been his favorite time of the year. The whole season, once holly and jolly, actually annoyed him. Ron didn't want a tree or decorations; he didn't want mistletoe or caroling. Instead, it all seemed to drive him further away from us, further away from *me*. Even Christmas music bothered him. He was not handling the news of this illness very well at all.

You see, Ron had a strong bond with his mom. He was the "favored one" in his family, and I often teased him that he was a mama's boy. Ron was always referred to as the "healing child," born to heal the wounds caused by the death of his brother, Eddie. At just eighteen months old, Eddie had ingested some poisonous chemical that ended up taking his life. Ron's mother, overwhelmed with grief and suffering from depression, visited the family doctor, who suggested she get pregnant again to overcome the pain and sorrow of Eddie's death. She conceived again, and Ron was born. So it wasn't surprising that the news of his mother's illness affected him so deeply.

As Ron watched his mother fade away and eventually die, I came to this realization: I am not a nurturer. I didn't know how to be there for Ron during this period. I couldn't reach out to him or even offer words of comfort. Instead, I would bark out orders:

"Shouldn't you be going to see your mom?"

"Don't you think you should call her instead of waiting for your sister to call you with updates?"

When his mom was moved to a hospital only four hours from us, I heard Ron telling his sister that he didn't have time to drive there. I knew it wasn't true, so instead of helping him sort through *why* he was saying he didn't have time, I told him that I had booked him a flight so he had no excuse. But again, I didn't do this with any form of compassion. I did it in a matter-of-fact way, knowing that it was the right thing to do. Ron went reluctantly, but even as I drove him to the airport he grew more and more quiet, more and more distant.

It's during these trying times that the true insecurities in our characters are revealed. Our weaknesses are most vulnerable during emotional times. I can't begin to tell you how often I have shared this fact with clients: Where there is high emotion, there is low intelligence. Those are the times when our hearts are not guarded. Ron would push through work, and I became numb.

I knew we were losing our connection, but as he withdrew, I could not push through the rejection I was feeling then, the rejection I felt when he gave me one-word answers to my questions and didn't take my hand as he always did when we were walking or driving. Soon, he forgot to kiss me good-bye when he left the house. He stopped calling me four or five times a day while he was gone, a habit of his that drove me nuts. (He told me that he just wanted to hear my voice.) That all stopped. Now I was shutting down, because somewhere in the mix, this had become about *him* not being there for me.

Any other nurturing woman would have known to be there for her husband during this trying season. It was then that I asked my friend to talk to Ron because I knew she understood the loss of a parent.

This is where I want to warn you, my readers, that most

affairs do not start in malice or with the intention of hurting anyone. Most affairs are birthed in pain and/or vulnerability, and that was the case for us. A fellow counselor once told me that vulnerability plus opportunity is the combination for most infidelity.

My pain and insecurity, coupled with the trauma of Ron losing his mother, left us susceptible to an attack on our marriage. At that time, I could feel the rock "walls" around my heart, walls that had slowly been built up over the years, rise higher, rock by rock.

Tearing Down the Walls

Pain is a great teacher, and people are smart. When something hurts, we usually learn to avoid it. When children touch a stove and get burned, they learn not to do it again. We're wired with the ability to feel pain in order to protect ourselves. However, we were never meant to put up permanent walls around our hearts—barriers that block out the bad *and* the good, walls that protect us from harm but also from feeling love.

Don't get me wrong; it's important to protect ourselves. But at the time we experience a wound, we usually put up walls instead of fences. When we're hurt, we need to put up fences with gates that we can swing open when we feel safe, just as we do with our homes. If you build big walls and create a concrete compound, you're going to live a lonely life. If you build a beautiful fence you can see through, you have the ability to make wise decisions about when and for whom you'll open your gate.

More times than not, people start putting up these walls as little children because they needed protection at one point and didn't get it. But at some point, we need to realize that we're not kids anymore and don't need to hide behind those walls.

It takes work to tear down the walls. It starts first with acknowledging that they are there. We need to identify the walls and what caused us to build them. This is the beginning of the *reveal* process.

When you allow God full access to your inner being and bring Him behind the walls that hide your broken, damaged heart, He will begin dismantling those walls, brick by brick, until the truth finally emerges.

All you need to do is to allow God entry, to give Him permission to show you the good, the bad, and the ugly of your choices. Believe me, God will show you the raw, unfiltered truth. He will show you how some of your past decisions have been made in the depths of pain, in the midst of the deepest kind of hurt—a level of hurt that is hard to imagine. But *we* can imagine it, can't we? We've been hurt. We've been betrayed, or on the other side, we've betrayed another.

I know what you're thinking: *Wait, I haven't betrayed anyone!* Well, that's not exactly true. The choices you've made out of hurt, anger, frustration, a hardened heart, or walls of distance will manifest through passive-aggressiveness, the silent treatment, and other behaviors. The simple truth is this: If allowed, God will reveal that we've all been hurt and we've all hurt people, and unfortunately, we usually hurt the people we love the most.

I had vowed never to nurture a man again, and I meant

it. That cup of coffee I wouldn't serve Ron, the affection I refused to show, and the intimacy I'd avoid or never initiate were ways I demonstrated the hurt and abandonment I'd felt as that twenty-one-year-old girl who had watched her boyfriend die of cancer. And as strange as this may sound, encouraging Ron would make me feel that he was *needy*, and I never handled *needy* well. Did I get to remain blameless when I knew my husband wanted, even *needed*, my attention?

Let's Go Even Deeper . . .

Protecting my heart from the unbearable pain of losing someone I deeply loved was a reasonable reaction, I thought. It was my right to be closed off and distant; it was my duty to guard my heart . . . after all, that's biblical! Wouldn't it have been borderline insanity for me to open myself up to such pain again?

At that point in my life, love equaled pain, and I vowed to protect myself at all costs. So I did the only thing I knew how to do: I created a wall around the most intimate part of my heart. The problem was, I never bothered to explain any of this to my husband. I never bothered to tell Ron *why* I would be closed off or *why* I wouldn't allow him access.

When you harden your heart, you use protective mechanisms, and in my case, it was closing off the caregiver in me. So when there was sickness, sadness, or weakness, my heart would harden and I would withdraw. Ron—and my kids, for that matter—never had the luxury of being nurtured or comforted when they were sick. That just wasn't me.

If I've heard it once, I've heard it a hundred times, mainly from my oldest daughter: "Mom! I just need you to be a *mom!*" Jenny was desperate to be loved, to be sympathized with, and to have a partner to commiserate with her. I would often hear, "I need you to just hug me or feel sorry for me or make me a cup of soup." If only it were that easy. It wasn't. My vow made acting that way risky; it was a much deeper issue than merely heating up soup or lying down for a hug with my sick kid.

I convinced myself that nurturing didn't come easily to me, that I wasn't made that way when, in reality, that was not at all true. The vow I'd made in the midst of my greatest pain had turned off my nurturing instincts just as you would turn off a water tap.

My Vow

What is a "vow"? A vow is described as a solemn promise. It can be a statement defined by the words "never" or "always."

I will never be hurt like that again.

I will never let a man control me again.

I'm never going to trust a friend again.

You get the idea. These are incredibly powerful statements with intense emotions attached. These are vows to avoid at all costs. Evil vows actually become sinful. Vows made in haste out of hurt or pain, anger or resentment, are vows that lead us astray.

The vow I made to close my heart was not a vow made to God; it was made in my own heart. It was a vow I had to break so I could be free to love my husband and children with my whole heart again. God, with His grace and my obedience and willingness, was able to show me how I had sinned out of my own personal hurts. Matthew 19:8, which happens to be the verse that our Relationship Lifeline ministry is built upon, defines the very sin that could have cost me my marriage: "He said to them, 'Moses, because of the hardness of your hearts, permitted you to divorce your wives, but from the beginning it was not so'" (NKJV).

The hardness of heart that Jesus spoke of entered my life as I saw my boyfriend in that casket. I'm so thankful to Jesus for His unending patience with us. In hindsight, I can see how God had tried to show me my sin in this area long before the affair happened, but I never perceived it.

I don't have to tell you how high a price I paid for my vow to never nurture a man again. It almost cost me everything: my marriage, my relationship with my kids, and my relationships with extended family. The gift of repentance that gave me a second chance still counts as one of my most prized blessings.

Revealing the vow and all its poison was the only reason my marriage ever received a second chance. The reveal process demanded acceptance and repentance. I had only myself to blame. Only I could take responsibility, apologize, and change.

Rewriting the vow meant I promised to trust God with all my heart. It meant I couldn't allow hurts, offenses, guilt, shame, or disappointments to drive me to the point of making another unhealthy vow in order to protect myself from hurt or fear.

Here's the truth: If we're alive in this world, we will be hurt, and probably more often than any of us would like.

The good news is that God will always be by our side. He is our constant Protector. He will be the one keeping the hurts from overwhelming us. Once I really understood that God had my heart and I could totally trust Him, the pressure was off.

Ron's Vow

When we first made the decision to fight for our marriage, to work toward healing for the both of us, well-meaning friends or caring family members would ask me: "How will you ever trust him again? Don't you know the old saying, 'Once a cheater, always a cheater'?" The question did haunt me, but not because I thought Ron would have another affair. I knew my husband was not a womanizer. However, I did worry he would go back to *her*. I knew this affair had not resulted from a sexual attraction but from a heart attraction.

Ron had never been nurtured by me. So when my friend, "the other woman," nurtured him during one of his most trying and painful times—the death of his mom—she touched his heart in a profound way, a way that I, up to that point, never had.

When I essentially forced Ron to visit his sick mother, I thought I was being helpful. I reasoned I would carry the load of work while he was gone. I'd be a good, sturdy wife and allow him time away to tend to this matter. Everything I did was done out of my desire to fulfill our biblical obligation to attend to our parents, especially when they can't take care of themselves. However, none of what I was doing came from a nurturing heart of compassion or empathy.

It was generated out of obligation. I was going by the law and how I was raised. You honor your parents. Period. That's just how it was. The problem with this was that I overlooked his pain by focusing on obligation, the safer bet for me.

Meanwhile, Ron was hurting and withdrawing, and my friend understood his pain. The attraction between them was emotional, and that feeling of finally being nurtured was the beginning of Ron's trance and believing a false reality.

I later learned that Ron had also made a dangerous, poisonous vow. He vowed that when the temptation got too strong to resist, he would simply stop trying. "No regrets" was what he had promised himself. He had determined never to regret this feeling of being cared for and nurtured.

Like my poisonous vow, Ron's vow had to be broken as well, and it was. But make no mistake, it cost him a lot as well. It cost him emotionally, physically, and spiritually. The time it took to heal his heart and mine from this "hell on Earth" hurt us both enough that we knew we never wanted to go there again.

Trust God and Love People

Let's return to the burning question about my marriage: *How would I ever be able to trust my husband again?* No matter what arguments I made in my head, I couldn't answer that question, at least not with any feeling of satisfaction or peace. At that point, I couldn't imagine how I *could* ever trust him again. I couldn't imagine how I could ever trust *anyone* again. So I prayed. I believe in a God who speaks, and I knew His voice. I've heard from God before, but this time when I prayed there was nothing but silence, and that silence was deafening.

In the weeks that followed, Ron refused to go to church. Shame was driving his entire life. I couldn't go either, but one particular Sunday I woke up feeling the sense that I needed to go. I got ready, but instead of wearing my Sunday best, another law-abiding habit from my upbringing, I decided to go in jeans and a hoodie. Obviously, hiding was my intention.

I made sure to arrive more than fifteen minutes late to ensure the foyer was empty, and my plan was to leave early. I walked into this place that only days earlier had felt like a second home, full of warmth and comfort, forgiveness and solace, where you greeted everyone and everyone greeted you back. But now it seemed strange, uncomfortable, and the opposite of what it was before. What had changed? I had, of course. I sat in the last row with my hoodie up, making sure to cover my head. No one needed to know I was there. It wasn't long before the pastor started his message, and then the oddest thing happened.

In the middle of his message, the pastor stopped mid-sentence and said, "I'm not sure why I need to stop right now and say this. It's not in my message, and it doesn't even make sense to me, but I'm certain that someone here needs to hear this." Here are the words God gave him to speak directly to me: "God never told us to trust people; He instructed us to *trust God* and *love people!*"

There was the answer to my prayer, clear as day! I left church right after he said that. I left that building laughing, crying, and rejoicing! On that day, I got my answer, but more importantly, I got peace, the peace that can only come from our God, who is always faithful. God came knocking on the closed, padlocked door of my heart, and I opened it from the inside. I let Him in, and I left the door open. To this day, and probably until the day I die, I will thank God for my pastor. He did something most are too busy to do: He stopped, and he listened!

My point in telling you this story is to encourage you. Remember those wristbands I mentioned a while back? The ones kids get at children's camp as a simple reminder to watch for God? Yes, it's just like that. Watch for God. Don't miss His still, small voice! Stay tuned to His voice and to His leading at all costs. I thank God I didn't listen to my shame or weakness telling me to stay away from church that day. I'm glad I watched for God. Those four simple words my pastor spoke—"Trust God. Love people"—changed the course of my healing and, more importantly, shut the enemy up on that haunting subject. There were other hardships, but when you watch for God, you'll find that He always has your back!

Now is a good time for you to stop and take a breath. If, on the other hand, you feel empowered and ready to continue climbing up your healing ladder, you can do that also.

First, take time to review this chapter. Find a quiet space, grab a pen, and ask yourself this hard question:

Is there a possibility that somewhere in my past I made a vow because of hurt or anger, promising never to be hurt again, never to trust again, or always to protect myself from _____ (fill in the blank)?

If this is the case, accept that this vow is wrong, and repent. Your vow has undoubtedly played a part in your current situation. Sinful vows wreak havoc. That is what they do. If this speaks to you, write those vows down and release yourself from them once and for all. The vow you need is the one where you promise to follow Jesus with all your heart, with all your mind, and with all your strength.

5

Spiritual Damage

THE AIR STARTED *to warm. Spring was clearly approaching, and with it, the promise of sunshine. On this Vancouver day, the sun soothed me in a way I desperately needed.*

Emotionally, I was spent. Five months of post-affair life and two moves later, I was done! The first move was strategic and planned. We needed to remove ourselves from our proximity to the other couple. We lived in a small community, attended the same church, and frequented the same grocery stores. It was a good decision for our healing. We chose northern California, since we could work from there and had a network of friends and spiritual leaders to help us restore our relationship.

The next move was definitely not planned and not even welcomed. Just five months after we'd moved to northern California, my father was diagnosed with cancer and given only a few months to live. With this new information, we once again packed up and headed back to the house we still owned in White Rock, British Columbia, and then made a permanent move to Vancouver.

I knew we needed help after our return to Vancouver. Once you experience what it feels like to be loved and nursed back to anything even close to normal health, you want more of the same. In California, we'd found some excellent marital and spiritual help from a pastor who really was the hands and feet of Jesus.

We wanted to continue to work on our marriage and remain accountable to people we respected and trusted, so Ron and I had discussed reaching out to the pastor of the church we'd been attending since our return home. This pastor was not our pre-affair, home-church pastor, but rather a pastor who had supported our ministry at one time. We assumed he would help us get our marriage back on track and also help us keep the ministry going. As we would quickly learn when we met with him, this was not at all the case.

A meeting with him seemed like a divine appointment, since just as we were planning to contact him, he reached out to us. So while I felt sick to my stomach about the meeting because I knew how much we had disappointed this pastor, I was still looking forward to seeing him and hopefully getting some encouragement and guidance. Little did I know that the pastor also wanted to talk to us about another issue.

We had decided to put our children in Christian school after we returned home from California, and one of the requirements for the reduced price was not only attending the church but also becoming members. When I heard the words, "I'm sorry we cannot approve your membership," I could hardly process them with my heart. Wow! Talk about a gut punch. But there was more.

"Also, we would really appreciate it if you did not attend the church."

All I could think was, Is he serious? I was completely morti-fied. I looked over at Ron, expecting that he would have some-thing to say about this. What I saw hurt more than anything that pastor could ever say to me. Ron's head was hanging low, the shame and humiliation almost too much for him to bear.

With my head held high and without any shame about the decision Ron and I had made to renew our marriage, I asked, "Are we being kicked out?"

The pastor answered, "Like I already said, your presence is really disturbing some of our members, and they are having a hard time worshiping."

It was then that my emotions got the better of me. I was more than a little angry, and to say I was rude would be an under-statement. After my outburst, I said, "I want you to put it in writing—the reasons we are being kicked out."

His response was, "In my thirty-plus years of ministry, I have never asked anyone to leave. I will not ask you to leave unless you choose to go, but I am sorry, we will have to refuse membership."

This pastor also suggested that Ron step down from the leader-ship of our ministry, which we were actually okay with, but that would leave me operating the ministry by myself—something that simply seemed impossible. If Ron was to step down for a season, I would need this pastor to support the ministry and help me. This was something he refused to do unless I divorced my husband for committing adultery. Needless to say, this was not an option I was willing to consider.

All I could do was look at this pastor—who apparently felt as if he was between a rock and a hard place—and say, "I am so sorry you don't believe in our marriage surviving this storm, but I thank God every day that my husband and I are together. We are going to fight for our marriage. Maybe it's too soon for you to imagine how this will turn out, but one thing I know is that our children deserve committed parents. They deserve to know their parents are fighting to keep this family together."

When we left that meeting, the sunshine no longer felt warm on my back, but Ron gave me one proud look! We chose each other, our marriage, and our family, even when our religious leader didn't believe in us. We kept our kids in the Christian school, paid full price, and God provided, despite the less than ideal circumstances.

———— •◆• ————

After spending my lifetime in churches, I considered myself a rare breed because I'd never been hurt by leadership and pastors. We had sailed along just fine until my husband had his moral failure. It was at this time that we needed spiritual support the most. Nonetheless, this is when I experienced the deepest pain and rejection I had ever known from leadership.

Not everyone was against us in our spiritual community. For instance, our pre-affair Canadian pastors were praying for Ron and me, as well as for our family as a whole. They stood with us, believing for our restoration, always lifting us up and encouraging us in that direction.

At times, it can seem like there is no end to the damage from this type of marital crisis, and that is exactly what the enemy would have us all believe. But I want you to take heart: Our God is a big God, and no amount of damage is too much for Him. But in my experience, spiritual damage is the most invasive and destructive type of damage one can incur. Spiritual damage attacks our hearts and our spirits, the core of who we are.

Until my husband's affair, I had no idea what true spiritual damage felt like. Until then, I had trusted most spiritual leaders. Like many people, I accepted that they also made mistakes, but I always assumed that their intention was not to harm me or the people they were tasked with shepherding. Unfortunately, that all changed after the affair.

The pastor who wouldn't support our ministry unless I divorced Ron went out of his way to convince me that I not only had the biblical right to leave my marriage, but that ending my marriage was the best thing I could do, not only for myself but also for our ministry. You can imagine my shock and dismay.

I can tell you that this was the most hurtful spiritual experience I have ever had to go through. It seemed to me that saving the ministry was more important to this leader than saving my family, and *that* was devastating. He told me that if I left my husband, he would help me save the ministry. I was completely dumbfounded by his reasoning.

When I went to this leader, I was scared, and I trusted him to help me. I desperately wanted to hear him say that he was there for Ron and me, for whatever we needed. Instead, what came back to us was an ultimatum: "Divorce Ron, or I will withdraw my support." His support to our ministry was substantial.

I was so certain that I had made it clear that I knew my marriage could be saved and that we had already made the decision to stay together. We just needed help walking through the repair work. Instead, this leader insisted that I had the biblical as well as the legal right to leave. The entire situation was heartbreaking. It was awful to hear this advice from a spiritual leader I admired and was relying on for help, and I was so angry that he wasn't supporting our efforts to heal our marriage.

Yet with time, those feelings softened, and relationships were healed because of God's amazing grace and forgiveness on both sides.

Needless to say, I ignored that advisor and didn't ask for a divorce. Instead, I chose not to look back but to fight with every ounce of energy I had in me to save my marriage—no matter what opposition we might face. God gave us the hope we needed, and we were going to lean on Him alone if need be.

Please know that for the most part, spiritual leaders are acting in what they believe to be a person's best interests. They're doing the best they can, the best they know how. In our case, however, this leader was clearly misguided.

I hope that no matter who suggests otherwise, you'll consider forgiveness and restoration before anything else. Try to keep the "breakup" and "divorce" rhetoric out of the situation and focus on allowing God to do His work. Someone saying you have the right to end your marriage—even if that someone is a respected spiritual leader—doesn't mean it's the right choice for you. According to the law in New Testament times, people had the right to stone the woman caught in adultery. But when Jesus pointed out their own sin, not one person picked up a stone.

Always strive to be kind and compassionate, no matter what response you may encounter. Lean on God's Word because it will never return void. A verse you'll see repeated in these pages (simply because it bears repeating) is Ephesians 4:32: "Be kind to one another, tenderhearted, forgiving one another, as God in Christ forgave you."

Marriages can't always be saved—I understand that—but restoration should be the first and only option for a while, anyway. Both people need to be doing everything humanly possible to stay together, all the while focusing on God and believing in His divine intervention. The only exception to this, of course, is if there's domestic abuse. If this is your situation, I would advise you to get safely away immediately. You cannot and should not put yourself, and especially your kids, in harm's way. Ever. For anyone.

You may be surprised to hear that in our weekend workshops, it's not our goal to keep couples from divorcing. It's our goal primarily to get individuals healthy and walking in forgiveness before they make any life-altering decisions. When you and your partner are healthy mentally, emotionally, and spiritually, you'll make healthy decisions. Divorce might be a healthy decision, but not if that decision comes from an angry, unforgiving, hurting heart.

I urge you to be encouraged because even if you feel that you'll never get healthy, God is faithful. Cry out to Him and ask Him to heal your heart! Start with that, and then begin to change what you can change.

The Power of Healthy Change

Unlike us, you may not be able to pack up everything and leave your country, state, or even city; however, everyone can change *something*. Change can be incredibly healing, even cathartic. I didn't realize why at the time, but from the beginning, I felt a need to change my surroundings as much as I could. I changed things in my home, moved the furniture, rearranged my closets, and even changed my bedding. I had a deep need to make things different. We even frequented different places. Change is good, so change what you can. The changes don't need to be monumental either. Even small changes will help you avoid stumbling into things that act as mental or physical triggers or negative reminders of the past.

Of course, it's hard to know who or what might be triggers for you because I don't know where you are in your journey of healing. What I do know is this: The sooner you start your journey toward renewal, the sooner healing and restoration will allow your heart to find the freedom it desperately seeks.

I had to set some things in motion early in my walk through what literally felt like the valley of the shadow of death. A lot had to die, not just in my husband, but also in us both before we could find redemption and move forward. But we were both committed to walking it out hand in hand, with the hope of a resurrected marriage and a brand-new, greatly improved life together.

Another Grief

We had planned to live in northern California for about a year while we healed. When our time away was cut short by the news of my father's illness, I again questioned God.

Honestly, God? How much more pain can I absorb?

The discovery of the affair five months prior to my dad's illness had created a total state of unrest in my heart.

And now my father is dying? I thought. What about that often-repeated "truth" that God won't give you more than you can handle? By the way, I'm now of the mind-set that God routinely gives us more than we can handle without Him so we learn to lean on and trust Him.

My dad was the most important male figure in my life, so much so that I looked for someone like him to be my husband. Ron was a blond, blue-eyed Russian version of my dark, brown-eyed Italian father. Now both of my strong towers appeared to be crumbling. In my heart, I truly believed that God wouldn't take my father at that time. *He just can't*, I thought. *That's way too much.* Nevertheless, within five months of our moving back to Canada, my father was gone.

It was grief upon grief, but I had to get out of my bed, out of my pit of darkness, and face my life. And wouldn't you know it, even with the heartache of my dad's passing, God made a way for me to find love and acceptance. Granted, maybe I didn't find it in the expected place— within the church body or its leadership. Instead, God led me to loving members of the body of Christ. Our support ultimately did come from Christ by way of His followers.

I came to understand that the pastors who hurt me were also hurt by what they had to face. Our failure caused them conflict. We also had to realize that we had put them in a hard position as pastors.

Last Resort

It's important to remember that pastors and elders are only people trying to serve in the best way that they know how. They are not a substitute for total reliance on our heavenly Father.

It's also important to remember that you are never really alone. No matter how you feel at this or any moment in the future, you'll never have to face a crisis on your own. Jesus promises to be with us, always. Lacking support from some religious leaders only served to strengthen our reliance on Jesus. We couldn't look to man for a way out of this nightmare. I'd strongly suggest you do as we did and rely on Jesus.

But be careful not to lump all of your spiritual leaders or counselors into one category. Align yourself with people who are *for* you, *for* your marriage, and *for* your family. Find people who will keep you accountable to the vision of a healthy marriage and family when the road gets rough, and especially when you may want to give up.

I have no way of knowing if you are ready for these next steps or not, but I'll share them with you anyway, trusting that God will guide you in His perfect timing.

Now brace yourself, and get ready for some thought-provoking work and an action plan. In the next section, I lay out the details of what needs to come next in your journey back to yourself and a healthy marriage.

PART TWO:
REWRITE

6

It's Time to Rewrite

ONE MIGHT THINK *that it's impossible to forgive the sin of infidelity, that cheating on your spouse is the ultimate, unpardonable iniquity. Strangely enough, forgiveness took only moments for me once I saw Ron a short twenty-four hours after hearing him say, "Yes, it's true."*

I had flown from Vancouver, where Ron and I lived at that time, to the small city of Trail, his childhood home where he was visiting his father. Ron picked me up at the airport with his father and sister in the vehicle. I noticed that Ron sat up front with his dad, who was driving, while I was relegated to the backseat with his sister. Looking back, I think this arrangement was Ron's way of protecting himself; maybe he thought I had arrived bearing arms, wishing to harm him. I'm sure the thought had probably crossed my mind twenty-four hours earlier!

The thirty-minute drive back to his father's house was quiet. There would be no small talk this time as we made our way through the city streets, and I'm sure Ron's dad and sister could feel our coolness toward each other. From the moment I entered the car, I realized that this drive wasn't the time or place to put more of a burden on his dad. After all, he'd just lost his wife of nearly fifty years to cancer the week prior. So we drove along in silence except for a few quiet exchanges between his sister and me in the backseat.

Forgiveness leaves an indelible mark on your soul. When forgiveness takes place, you know that a miracle has just transpired. I'm not sure if it's normal to feel this way the moment forgiveness descends on you. But it happened to me, and I know exactly when it occurred. Forgiveness came the second Ron walked my suitcase into the bedroom, took me in his arms, and held me tight. I melted. At that moment, I forgave my husband. I remember that my whole body lost strength, and I was like a rag doll in his embrace. I was washed over with forgiveness. I wish I could tell you that my pain went away at that exact moment as well, but I assure you it didn't. That pain would last for what felt like an eternity.

The decision to restore my broken marriage took days, but the process to renew my marriage was a two-year walk through the deepest agony I'd ever faced. Honestly, the first six months were the worst. There was screaming and yelling. There was the throwing of all his things out of the master bedroom closet. There was crying and praying, pushing each other away and pulling each other back in. Eventually, laughter returned and our lives were healed.

Restoration and healing didn't come easily to Ron and me, but I would do it all over again because what followed was a great gift: the start of another twenty years together. And it all began with the gift of forgiveness I offered Ron that night—the most valuable thing I'd ever given.

The Scarlet Cord

I've just shared my story about forgiving Ron, but what about "the other woman"? To be honest, if I allowed myself to think about the situation from a human perspective, I would be entirely justified to hate her, despise her, and blame it all on her. I wanted to think of this woman who had called herself my best friend as a despicable home-wrecker and a lowlife.

But I knew deep inside that this was not the truth, and I also knew that this line of thinking would not bring healing to my life or marriage. We're tasked to look at Jesus and to think about the grace and forgiveness afforded us through His sacrifice on the cross. We must face the horrible things we, too, have done to others, even if it's not adultery. There are times we've also been unlovable.

In Joshua 2, two Israelite spies asked Rahab, the prostitute, for a place to hide. A red cord symbolized that she was a prostitute. This same red cord saved her and her family on the day of her city's destruction because she had faith in the Israelites' God. Despite her sin and shame, God loved Rahab and saved her.

Her story made me stop and be honest with myself about

my own situation. I also reread the story of the woman at the well in John 4. This woman was scorned and could not go to the community well until the heat of noonday because of her shame; she wanted to avoid the other women who drew water early in the day. I read about how Jesus treated her, how He approached her, and I thought to myself, *Am I caught in my own shame for thinking of myself as better or worth more than my friend?* Then I turned to the story of the woman caught in adultery in John 8. Jesus turned this woman's accusers away. Not one of these women had any right to expect mercy, yet they all received it. Every one of them had done wrong, yet God extended grace to them.

If you've been hurt by someone, or if someone has taken your spouse, I understand the anger you feel. I've felt it. I understand the hatred. I've felt it. I understand the sense of betrayal. I've felt it. But like me, you have to decide if hatred will serve you. Hatred for the other woman or man will not only continue to destroy your marriage, but it will also eventually destroy your soul. It will eat away at you from the inside out. When we fall short of the grace of God, a root of bitterness can set in that will ruin us and everyone around us. It will cause trouble and corruption in everything we do. The Bible says it this way in Hebrews 12:15: "Look after each other so that not one of you will fail to find God's best blessings. Watch out that no bitterness takes root among you, for as it springs up it causes deep trouble, hurting many in their spiritual lives" (TLB).

If we lose grace, we allow a root of bitterness to grow inside us that not only defiles us but also—according to that verse—defiles many. Could it be that the "many" God is speaking about are your children or your extended family? Or perhaps even those within your sphere of influence? I believe this to be true. I also believe that the "root of bitterness" could cost you your purpose and possibly even your life's calling. That is a monumental price to pay to hate someone. I know for Ron and me, it could have cost us all those things.

I thank God every day that He gave me the strength to forgive my husband *and* the "other woman" because that allowed me to experience God's grace in my own life. The "other woman," now my friend again, not only saved my marriage but hundreds of others through our collective story of grace.

The Gift of Grace

I was able to show grace to others because there had been times in my life when others showed grace to me. Reflect on this as you read this book. God will help you keep your heart soft; He will help keep that bitter root from setting in and taking control. Just remember Hebrews 12:15 and don't fail to receive grace for yourself or give grace to others, if for no other reason than your own mental and emotional well-being.

I believe 100 percent that my own story would not have ended the same if I hadn't experienced the grace of God before this happened. If I failed to extend that same grace to others who had so badly hurt me, would I not then be a hypocrite? The Bible teaches us that as we have freely received, we should now freely give (see Matthew 10:8).

Remember that grace is a gift: It is never deserved or earned, and it is always available and accessible. The freedom gained from embracing this truth in your journey will open the floodgates of healing for you just as it did for me. "The other woman" or man can be the catalyst for saving your marriage, and the end result will be that you will *renew* your marriage and your life, making it better than it ever was before.

If you refuse grace, anger and unforgiveness will remain like a wedge between you and your healing, and you will face a losing battle. It's impossible to heal a hardened, closed-off heart. Your decision needs to be a complete and full surrender, with you on your knees before God saying, *I'll do anything, whatever it takes, to take my life back.* This needs to be your prayer.

When I uttered the words, "God, heal me," I trusted that He *would*; believe that as well. If you trust and surrender, God will heal you. Believe me, He healed me. God is the *only* One who can heal your broken heart. As it says in Psalm 51:17, "A broken and contrite heart, O God, you will not despise."

God can and will forgive you, but what He can't do is forgive others for you. If you're anything like me, you have no idea how you will ever be able to heal from something this devastating. You probably have no idea how you'll ever be able to turn your heart of stone into a heart of compassion and forgiveness for yourself, your spouse, *or* "the other woman" or man.

This may well be your question right now: *What if I don't want to forgive? What if I can't forgive?*

Freedom through Compassion

We tend to think of forgiveness as something done on behalf of the person who wronged us, and it can be that . . . but it's also so much more. Forgiveness can be more important for you than for the person you're struggling to forgive. Forgiveness is about freeing yourself from the tremendous pain and overbearing weight that you've been carrying since you were hurt. Forgiveness is undoubtedly hard, but when it's accomplished, it can be immensely powerful to the point of feeling miraculous.

Forgiveness is really about allowing yourself to heal and move forward in freedom—even if reconciling with those who hurt you isn't an option. I want to help you understand the forgiveness process as it focuses internally on your health and future. I want to help you let go and be free.

Don't be discouraged; God can help you do this just as He helped me. I knew there was no way I could forgive and be free on my own. I had absolutely no thoughts of compassion toward "the other woman." My heart was full of anger, which produced severe thoughts of hurting her with my words—something I eventually did when I had the opportunity.

At some point, you come to realize that this behavior does no good. It doesn't make you feel better, and it certainly doesn't help the other person. Even more importantly, it doesn't please God.

As Christians, we are not called to hold tightly to unforgiveness. Realizing this one day, I got down on my knees and prayed: *Jesus, give me the compassion the Father gave to You for those who hurt You. Lord, You know I'm like Peter when he lashed out, angry and hurt, and cut off the ear*

69

of the soldier trying to arrest You. Your reaction was to restore. You simply healed the soldier's ear on the spot. I want to be Peter right now. Every ounce of energy I have in me wants to really hurt her, make her feel a small taste of the hurt she has given to me. But I know this is wrong, so please help me.

As quickly as I uttered this prayer, the Lord answered, and a surge of compassion came over me. I know it sounds crazy, but isn't that how our God works? Isn't the Bible filled with stories of amazing grace and awesome power? I'm not sure why this constantly surprises us, but it surely surprised *me.*

Can you consider doing what I did? I encourage you to stop reading right now and pray that same prayer. Just take a quick moment: Stop. Breathe. Pray. Settle your mind and your heart, and allow God to show you His compassion, just as He showed me.

Forgiving "the Other Woman"

Within seconds of that prayer, a remarkable wave of peace and compassion swept over me. Then the phone rang. I was in my home office alone. I took the call and it was my friend, "the other woman." Her voice was soft and sorrowful.

Isn't that just like God? He delivered, and in that moment, it was as if He was saying, "Tina, are you serious? Are you really after a heart of compassion? Because if you are, here is your opportunity; here is where you get to start."

To say that God had a strange way of answering my prayer would be an understatement for sure. Was He really using "the other woman" to begin my healing?

When we open our hearts and allow Him to use us and

heal us, God sometimes takes us down mysterious avenues. All He needs is our permission to do whatever is necessary, and I can tell you from experience, He will do it.

As strange as it might seem, just the sound of her voice was healing to me. She was still the kind, nurturing friend she had been for years. The difference now was that her voice was not joyful. She hadn't called to tell me a story or to make me laugh, as she had so many times before. Instead, this was a voice of shame and remorse. I could feel her pain. She knew very well the destruction she and my husband had caused both of our families.

The Process Begins

This phone call was the beginning of the healing process that would take months and years to play out. Make no mistake, the road ahead was not easy for any of us just because we now had compassion one for another. The months ahead took us on a roller-coaster ride, and it wasn't a fun one.

Many times, it felt like our cars on this ride had some loose screws and were all beat up from crashing. Indeed, there were times when it felt as if crashing was the only possible outcome. It was as if someone had tampered with the brakes and we all were left to careen out of control toward the inevitable disastrous end. In those times, I had no choice but to put my faith in God's promises, for example, Psalm 27:13-14 (NKJV): "I would have lost heart, unless I had believed that I would see the goodness of the LORD in the land of the living. Wait on the LORD; be of good courage, and He shall strengthen your heart; wait, I say, on the LORD!"

I felt like I was losing heart, and you might be feeling that way too; you might be feeling faint or full of despair as some other Bible translations of this verse state. I felt all of it, everything listed in every translation of that passage.

I believed death would have been better than what I was feeling those first few months, but I had to trust and *wait* on the Lord. Because I was able to wait and find courage, God gave me peace and, slowly but surely, He did strengthen my heart. God has promised to do far more than we could ask or think of Him, but we must trust in His goodness and that He will turn things in our favor.

The Giant Eraser

Like me, you might be thinking that it would be so much easier to forgive if you could simply erase from your mind the memory of the painful experience. I certainly thought that more than once.

One day God graciously gave me exactly what I needed: a vision, a *knowing* on the inside. This was the vision: The ceiling opened, and I saw an outstretched hand offering me a giant eraser. Divinely, I received a revelation. I knew that I was being handed a once-in-a-lifetime opportunity. I was being given a way to erase every painful memory from my lifetime to that point. I knew the eraser would be able to eradicate all of my inner "thought" demons, to block all of the bad memories and make it as if these horrible, scarring events had never happened. The giant eraser would instantaneously clean everything away into the sea of forgetfulness.

Then I heard an instructor I hadn't noticed before shout,

"One minute!" I was suddenly aware of my surroundings in this vision. We were attending a marriage weekend seminar, and the instructor was clear I had one minute to use my new magic eraser. And boy, was I ready to use it! My mind started racing through all the memories that haunted me, all the things that, if they popped into my head for even a second, could ruin my day or worse. I was definitely ready.

After I snatched that eraser out of the hand coming from the open ceiling, all of the memories materialized on an impossibly long dry-erase board. I placed the eraser on the first one—the day I said good-bye to my grandmother. No, I wouldn't start there. I was sure there was an even more painful memory to erase first.

I quickly went on to the day I was laughed at after coming out of the boys' bathroom. Yes, that would be the one. I knew that as I worked forward in chronological order there would be other memories to dwarf this one. Yet this was as good a place as any to start my memory makeover!

I was ready to begin, so I placed the eraser on the board . . . yet for some reason, the eraser wasn't making contact with the board. Nothing was being removed. Instead, I felt a crazy rush of time passing—it seemed like a Star Trek teleporter dropped me off right in front of the affair! I would have ended up there eventually: It surely was one of the most painful memories—if not *the* big kahuna of painful memories—and of course I wanted to erase it. In fact, I wanted nothing more! Now I could remove it, wipe it out, annihilate it. But I didn't. Instead, I reached up and gave the giant eraser back to the hand in the open ceiling. *What?* I couldn't believe I had done that. I didn't remove *anything*—not one painful memory—and trust me, there were tons to choose from, including memories I'd prayed for years to have removed.

I returned the eraser and didn't alter one thing across the span of my entire life's storyboard. Feeling completely exhausted, I exhaled an exasperated sigh, my tears flowing.

I realized that erasing any part of my story would change everything.

Our ministry.

Gone.

Our home.

Gone.

My children.

Gone.

The miraculous adoption of our daughter Mia.

Gone.

Our purpose and dream to heal relationships, one broken heart at a time.

Gone.

Changing one thing can change everything. God's miracle of life weaves everything together so tightly. Your story, all of your story, is who you are.

I also realized, based on past experiences, that God had already begun turning the affair into a story, a testimony of healing that wasn't only for our family but also for many others. God says we overcome the enemy through our testimony: "And they have conquered him by the blood of the Lamb and by the word of their testimony, for they loved not their lives even unto death" (Revelation 12:11).

As you work on forgiveness and the rewriting of your story, remember that God can, and most likely will, use your story for His glory. We have no idea what the impact of our efforts toward change will be. A pebble tossed into a calm lake creates ripples that spread far and wide. The same thing can happen with the renewing of your own story.

7

Guarding against
a Hard Heart

WE FINALLY BEGAN *having good days, and I could feel my heart starting to soften. Sacramento had proven to be a good move for our collective healing. The rewrite of our lives was in full action, and I was feeling loved more than ever. I hadn't had a nightmare in days, our lovemaking was healing us both, and my guard was down.*

One day Ron and I were meeting with a couple to help them build their own seminar company when my phone rang. I answered the call and immediately wished that I hadn't. I was told that my husband had contacted "the other woman."

I excused myself and walked out of the training room, trying to control my breathing. My entire body reacted with nausea-driven convulsion, and I could almost feel my heart become rock-hard again. I was ready to march back into that training room and freak out! I didn't care if I embarrassed my husband in front of everyone!

I hung up the phone and walked back into the room. Ron must have noticed that I looked as white as a ghost because he quickly and gently escorted me out. I looked at him with total disdain and said, "Don't even try to lie to me. I just got a call saying you've been in contact with her!" I didn't take my eyes off his face; I needed to see his response as much as hear it.

"I don't know who just called you," Ron said, "but I haven't been in touch with her since that day five months ago when I told you that I choose you."

I wanted to believe him, but I couldn't risk it. For the next twenty-four hours, I went into investigative mode and called our cell phone company. I asked for a full report of the incoming and outgoing calls from Ron's phone. I needed answers right away.

He was telling the truth, thank God. Even so, I was rocked to the core. Seeing how quick I was to harden my heart toward my husband, I was forced to ask myself, Am I fooling myself? *I realized that I was all too ready to believe one of the enemy's many lies. I knew that I couldn't allow this kind of altercation to affect the condition of my heart anymore.*

———— ◆ ————

I am confident in God's promises of healing for you. However, what concerns me is how hearts can harden and how that hardness can build up. That resistance can derail you and prevent you from receiving the healing God promises in His Word. Remember what Matthew 19:8 says about this condition: "He said to them, 'Because of your hardness of heart Moses allowed you to divorce your wives, but from the beginning it was not so.'"

Matthew 19:8 is worth repeating because it's the foundation of our ministry to couples and individuals. All of human history shows us that when we are at our lowest, when we have hardened our hearts to the point of stone, God has the power to soften them, to open them back up to healing and to loving again. Just when an individual is prepared to cement his or her heart of stone, our God restores it to a soft, open, loving heart of flesh, a heart that is open to forgiving and to forgiveness, a heart that is open to receive all the goodness God promises.

I have experienced this firsthand. Since Relationship Lifeline was founded by my husband and me in 1995, we've seen thousands of broken hearts become wonderfully and even supernaturally healed, even though one spouse was prepared to abandon the relationship.

God wants all of us to have soft hearts. He wants supple hearts of flesh that long for His goodness and mercy, His grace and healing. He desperately wants to take our rock-hard, walled-up hearts and make them pliable again. He wants us to be like clay, easy to mold. Let Him be the potter—let His hands mold you back together.

I love the story in Ezekiel 11 where God wants to restore His people and gather them back to Himself. They've wandered dangerously far from Him, at their own risk. Does this sound like you or your spouse? Is your marriage teetering on a precipice, close to disaster? Or worse, does it feel as if it is already plummeting toward a catastrophic end that will hurt not only you but all those around you both?

Even if all of this seems to be true, God still cares deeply, unfathomably about you, your spouse, your circle, and the remains of your marriage. He hurts with you, cries with you, aches with you, and wants to heal you. He can work with the remnants of your shattered marriage. The Creator of the universe needs only your okay to change your life and the lives of those hurting with you or of those who hurt you. God wants to heal us individually as well as within the union of our marriage, and this is His promise in Ezekiel 11:17-19.

Let's start with verse 17, when God says, "and I will give you the land of Israel." In my interpretation, the land represents your life.

Your part of the deal is in verse 18: "And when they come there, they will remove from it all its detestable things and all its abominations." I understand this verse to mean that you will need to reveal all the rocks in your heart—the vows you've made that have hardened your heart.

Verse 19 clearly states God's promise to us: "I will give them one heart, and a new spirit I will put within them. I will remove the heart of stone from their flesh and give them a heart of flesh."

If you will trust Him and step out in faith by giving your stony heart and evil vows to God, and if you own *your* part of what you dragged into your relationship, I assure you that God will show you such amazing grace that it will leave you dumbfounded.

In our Relationship Lifeline weekends, it always breaks my heart when I hear stories of those unwilling to test God, to see if He will deliver on His promises. Some people believe they are unable to change or to see others change, which is the biggest lie the enemy puts in our heads. Another lie some have believed is that God can't help them—that they can't get better. The truth is, God has provided everything we need to do what is right. He has given us Jesus, who has promised to make what is impossible for us possible with Him.

Make no mistake, for those unwilling even to try to release their hard hearts, to trust God and obey Him, there are consequences. Consider Ezekiel 11:21: "But as for those whose heart goes after their detestable things and their abominations, I will bring their deeds upon their own heads, declares the Lord GOD."

Wow! That sounds serious and like an extremely high price to pay for hardening your heart, don't you agree? The Living Bible paraphrase and some other translations use the word *idols* in verse 21: "'But as for those now in Jerusalem who long for idols, I will repay them fully for their sins,' the Lord God says."

Let's examine what a stony heart full of idols or abominations looks like: It could be a prideful heart, a victim attitude, unforgiveness, or even knowing what is right but refusing to do it. When we harden our hearts, we risk God actually leaving us to our own choices, allowing us the full weight of the consequences we rightly deserve. This is the side of free will that no one brags about.

When we allow our hearts to grow hard, we will find ourselves having to live in unforgiveness. When we refuse to let go of anger, we have to live in the cloud of that same anger. It's important to be aware of what feelings you foster, as more often than not they will be what you receive in return. The boomerang effect is real.

If there was infidelity in your marriage, no doubt you're hurting. My plea is that you don't let that hurt keep you from looking to the ultimate Healer. My best years of marriage came only after I allowed God to reveal my hardened heart full of rejection, anger, resentment, hurt, shame, revenge, and evil vows. It was only then, in that moment of surrender, that He shined His light into my darkness.

It's hard to describe the relief and healing that occurred with God's light. God healed me and gave me a better life and a better marriage—more than I could have ever dreamed of.

But before I surrendered my hardened heart to God, I counted the cost. To an ultimate control freak like me, the cost of that surrender was to willingly put myself in a place of vulnerability, a place where I might once again feel immense pain. I wasn't sure that I wanted to risk being hurt that way a second time. We harden our hearts so we don't have to feel pain. But what God was asking me was to trust Him, which meant opening myself up to pain again. Pain indicates that something is wrong and needs healing. If we harden our hearts against that pain, we close ourselves off from Jesus' healing. In the end, even after counting the cost, I realized vulnerability was not a high price to pay for God's reward of a renewed life.

The Effects of Sin

My husband's affair caused me to judge "the other woman," which only served to harden my heart. God was asking me to let go of that judgment. I wanted to reserve the right to stay angry and unforgiving. Talk about total surrender! It would have been so much easier for me, especially at that time, just to continue blaming her. I wanted to believe she seduced my husband, that she was a flirtatious, evil woman who tempted my husband. I knew this wasn't true, but it surely would have been easier to believe the lie. The truth is this: It's actually unusual that affairs start by intending to destroy anyone or anything. This is where the interesting phenomenon of the trance comes in. This state of mind makes it easier for even the strongest men and women to behave in uncharacteristic ways.

Let's think for a moment about the person who has been involved with your spouse. In all likelihood, this person didn't plan to destroy you, your family, or his or her family (if that applies). The involvement was likely a case of old-fashioned temptation that was allowed to blossom. Like a single match that turns into a raging wildfire and destroys everything in its path for miles and miles, unchecked temptation is devastating. Not seeing the "out" door, the way of escape, can wreak more havoc on a marriage than most people can imagine. Except we *can* imagine it because we've lived it or are still living it. If temptation is left to blossom, powerful but short-lived feelings can deceive a sound mind and result in a "trance" mind-set. The trance is strong, cunning, clever, and incredibly powerful. We would all do well to be aware of and keep in close check our relationships with the opposite sex.

Another effect of sin came in the form of my now almost-constant nightmares. Every night for months, I would dream of my once-devoted husband looking at me indifferently and walking out the door, leaving me there to bleed. I'm not talking about vague, nonspecific "bad dreams." I'm talking about intense, vivid, full-blown nightmares. As if that wasn't bad enough, throughout the day I'd have random outbursts of "ugly cries." It was debilitating as well as frustrating.

Possibly the biggest price we paid because of this affair was the hurt we saw in our children's eyes. They had no idea what had happened to their happy home, to their loving parents, to their way of life. Because of what happened, we decided to move away from the small beach town of White Rock, British Columbia, where we had lived happily and comfortably for years. Our kids had to move to different homes, different schools, even a different country. They lost friends and had to start over at an age when starting over is incredibly difficult. I still consider this among the greatest consequences of the affair and its aftermath.

The choices you make now, in the midst of whatever you are going through, can have long-term negative effects on the innocent children caught in the mess we adults create.

During the first five months after the affair, we lived in Sacramento to help friends build their seminar business. It was a convenient way to escape our surroundings and our now-destroyed life. This one choice, painful but necessary for the adults, forced our children to be apart for the first time in their lives. Our oldest, Jenny, was fifteen and did not want to go to the States, so she decided to stay with her aunt. Joshua, our son, went with us since he was in fifth grade at the time. It was difficult for him to move from the home he grew up in and away from his friends to an American school. His problems after the move may have been more devastating for me than for him because it took me back to my own childhood pain. I was somehow reliving the pain of my early childhood through his trauma. (My parents, because of their unhappiness, moved my sister and me from a happy, safe place in Belgium all the way to Canada.)

Let's not fool ourselves: Sin has plenty of negative after-effects. Sin has a cost, and I can attest to the fact that it is high. Don't ever doubt that.

Ron told me that seeing the pain in my eyes was a memory forever stamped on his heart. Remembering that he was the one who had put that pain there would be a constant reminder of his selfish "no regrets" vow. His momentary thrill was not worth my pain, the pain he caused his children, and the guilt he believed he would carry for the rest of his life over the breakup of another marriage and the devastation he caused another family.

How to Soften a Heart

When you're dealing with these devastating effects of sin, how do you rewrite the state of your heart, which seems impossible to change?

Start by asking Jesus for His compassion, the kind of compassion He demonstrated on the cross of Calvary. Remember, in His darkest hour, during the deepest betrayal known to man, Jesus said, "Father, forgive them."

But did He end His statement there? No. He continued by saying, "For they know not what they do." I can still hear my husband's voice as he taught this very Scripture from dozens of stages across the U.S. and Canada. Why did Jesus say, "For they know not what they do"? Ron would say to rooms full of people, "Is it possible that Jesus was making an excuse for those who had beaten and crucified Him?"

We tend to think that we shouldn't make excuses for people we need to forgive. But maybe Christ's words are worth more investigation. Let me explain what I mean.

As I tried to forgive, I searched my soul, asking God to help me see the affair from a different perspective. God took me back to an earlier time at a job when a man's compliments made me feel good. Really good. So good, in fact, that I found myself desiring this man's compliments and attention. I would seek to sit next to him in meetings, make excuses to ask him for help, etc. Just as the apostle Paul warns us, we have incredibly weak flesh and an incredibly strong roaring lion of an enemy who seeks to devour us. I realized that, but for the grace of God, I could have ended up in a trance like my husband. I had no intention of having an affair and destroying my or anyone else's family, but it sure could have happened.

I know without question that my husband and friend did not call a meeting and discuss the ways they could hurt the people who trusted them. I know they didn't look at the long-term, big picture of their actions before the enemy planted the deceitful feelings that started growing. I am certain they had no plan to destroy me or her spouse or any of our kids.

Here's the point: It's time to give forgiveness a shot. If we believe what Jesus said on the cross, we can conclude that the people who hurt us really *didn't know what they were doing.* We know that the enemy had his claws deep into them.

I know where your head wants to go right now, but for

argument's sake, imagine your spouse's case as one of tempo-rary insanity. This doesn't let anyone off the hook, and the consequences are still real and devastating, but this change of perspective may allow you to move forward. Imagine that when your spouse and the other person first succumbed to the temptation of their affair, they fell into a trance. Recognizing my husband's trance was how my road to forgiveness started. Will you let it be how your road to forgiveness starts as well?

Let's remember that "all have sinned and fall short of the glory of God" (Roman 3:23). Even when we've sinned, we've seen God turn our shortcomings into something good. Let's press past the pain and believe the same for others, even for those who have wronged us.

Understanding a Hardened Heart

A hardened heart can begin in childhood as a reaction to painful events. Most likely, you don't even realize you've been gathering rocks to build that wall of protection inside your chest. My little heart was already full of rocks when I was eight and my parents decided to move from Belgium to Canada.

My grandma's house in Belgium was my safe haven. I could do anything at Grandma's—even get dirty and not get in trouble. Conversely, my parents' home was more like a museum. Strict rules were in place to keep everything neat and clean at all times. It was almost as if no one lived there. My grandparents doted on me. After all, I was their first grandchild.

While I felt as if I was a burden to my parents, I felt

the opposite at my grandparents' house. I had heard stories that my mom didn't want a baby. She was sixteen when she married my dad, and a baby was not on her wish list. At Grandma's, I was completely wanted and totally accepted and loved! I will never forget how I felt the day we moved, waving good-bye to Grandma after letting go of her hand. Talk about painful! That truly was all my little heart could take. For the second time, I was forced to say good-bye to grandparents before heading to an entirely new continent. I'd already had to leave my dad's parents, who lived in Italy and were my caretakers the first two years of my life.

My heart was heavy as we entered the plane. In addition to the rocks of rejection I felt from my mom's lack of affection and love, a new rock was being added to the growing pile: a rock called *loss*. That new rock would haunt me for years, and it was probably the rock that hardened my heart the most.

Loss was the heaviest rock and the one that made me feel physically sick. I spent the next eight hours of that plane ride throwing up into one of the little white bags. To this day, when someone talks about leaving me, or when I *think* someone I love might be leaving me, I get physically sick. That's how real these rocks are.

There is nothing metaphorical about the rocks—or baggage—in your life. The hardness of heart that made me physically sick way back then, and again when I found out about the affair, didn't actually leave me until I reclaimed my heart and allowed myself to feel again. That's when I was able to let go of my fear of nurturing others, to let go of my selfishness, and to tear down my wall of protection. Finally,

I was able to reach out to offer comfort and support, to nurture someone else. That is when my life changed.

Satan's Tricks

Never forget that your walls and defenses are things Satan will use to trick you. This all makes sense to me now. I had two significant losses early in life, so I felt justified in building the wall up around my heart. I had a right to protect and look out for myself, didn't I? Except I wasn't justified in doing that. The wall I created around my heart kept me from nurturing and caring for my husband in the way he needed me to.

The only way to truly live is to release your rocks and take a risk. There is no love without risk. There is no life without risk. So live! Risk. Love. Nurture. And remember that when you do these things for others, they will be done for you as well.

Now let's begin your journey of healing. The next section will help you start the R3 process that leads to healing. Step one is realizing this fact: It's up to you to *reveal, rewrite,* and *renew* your story!

Heart Work: The R3 Factor

Welcome to the R3 Factor. This is the start of something good, something new and refreshing. I promise you that not one exercise in the R3 Factor system will be a waste of time. Instead, the R3 Factor provides hope and a road map to healing, but you'll need to do the work.

Now let's get on with your recovery journey. Your journey will consist of three areas of focus, and it is important that you understand the purpose of each area. As you go through this process, you'll start to see how the scattered puzzle pieces of your life can fit together to create a new, even better picture.

So what exactly *is* the R3 Factor? The R3 Factor is a process that uses the principles of R1: Reveal (yesterday), R2: Rewrite (today), and R3: Renew (tomorrow).

Relationships break down not because love isn't there, but because of the baggage and the wounds dragged into current relationships from the past. It doesn't matter if your childhood was healthy or turbulent: Everyone has wounds. If something from your past is showing up in the present, the truth is, it's *not* in the past!

R1: Reveal

The first R1 (Reveal) is probably the most difficult part of the R3 Factor, yet it's your starting point. This is about yesterday. Believe it or not, yesterday has a lot to do with this traumatic situation you might now be facing. I wouldn't have believed it until I lived through it. But once I did, I was amazed at how much my *today* is based on my *yesterday*.

I know revealing the past is scary. It was scary for me then, and it continues to concern me to this day because—let's be honest—who wants to reveal all their secrets? Who wants to dig up the bones of old hurts and past losses? No one. At least no one I know or have counseled.

But here's why it matters: Without revealing your yesterday, you can't expect to have a better tomorrow. It's that simple. It is impossible for you to have a better present and future without looking backward first. Whether I'm speaking at our weekend workshops, churches, conferences, a seminar for the Marine Corps, in a celebrity's home, or on the *Today* show, I always say the same thing: "You cannot heal or change what you do not reveal."

The Oxford dictionary defines *reveal* as follows: to "make (previously unknown or secret information) known to others."[1] The basis for the reveal portion of our healing is to do exactly that—to make the unknown known. Once we do that, we can discern if we have hardened our hearts.

It's important to understand that none of us can escape hardness of the heart. That being the case, let's examine how our hearts become hard in our relationships with those we love.

At birth, your heart is like a clear jar; but as you journey through life, you pick up rocks. The rocks represent hurts, wounds, and negative experiences that have occurred throughout your lifetime. When these rocks are not dealt with, they become a rock wall built with anger, resentment, shame, and bitterness. You may falsely believe that you are protecting yourself from hurt, shame, and wounding, but you are actually creating within yourself an anxious and heavy heart. Proverbs 12:25 says, "Anxiety in a man's heart weighs him down."

Even so, people continue to go through life picking up rocks one at a time. Some are pebbles and some are boulders, some have jagged edges while others appear smooth on the surface, but all rocks have one thing in common: They are *hard*.

Have you heard the expression "Don't build walls around your heart"? Walls can provide protection, but they also isolate.

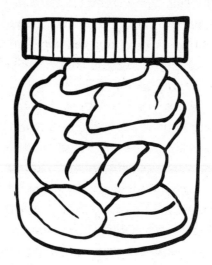

While the Bible clearly says that we are to "guard our hearts," it does not say that we are to *isolate* our hearts, to wall them off. The rocks of hurt, guilt, betrayal, addiction, or other pain can create an edifice that stands between you and the people you love. This is why the reveal process is so important; it allows us a way of acknowledging each rock so we can change our story and heal the hurts, one rock at a time.

It's vital that you understand this. Your past is not an out-of-sight, out-of-mind type of thing. That's not how our brains are wired. What happened yesterday, without question, affects today. You can't heal what you don't reveal. You need to develop an awareness of how you really feel and what is really going on inside. This involves your heart, the core of your being. Don't underestimate this step, and don't think this is something you can do in one afternoon and move on.

We are incredibly complex creatures, created with intention-ality and specificity. We are all works in progress, and this is part of the work. Revealing yourself, openly and honestly, is a never-ending process. As long as we draw breath, we will always have things to ponder and explore about ourselves.

You may be asking, "How do I do this? I don't even know where to begin." You begin with committing to total "uncomfortable honesty," as a friend of mine calls it. The goal here is to discover who we are and why we do what we do, and that can only be accomplished by being transparent. No one is watching. No one is scrutinizing. No one is judging. This is important, and it's the only way you can start to move past your hurt, shame, embarrassment, or anger.

Most people carry around secrets or issues from their past that they want to keep buried. Once buried, we avoid these old painful memories because we fear that they may not be fixed. But dealing with past wounds is vital to overcoming painful, present-day relational conflicts.

The unrevealed wounds and secrets that you saw, heard, and experienced as a child often become emotional buttons—triggers—in current relationships. Many issues that trigger a negative overreaction stem from negative child-hood events that have become rocks in your heart. For one person, the trigger is being late; for another, it's being overly upset about what someone says about her or him; and for yet another, it's getting lost while driving. When someone steps on one of your rocks, you get triggered, and you may have a reaction that is disproportionate to the offense. Start now to take notice of when someone or something triggers a nega-tive feeling and causes it to rise up inside of you.

Before you begin the following exercise, take time to:
Stop.
Breathe.
Pray.
Give God permission to reveal the rocks that have hardened your heart.

Reveal Exercise

Write on each rock one toxic emotion that it represents. Examples could be anger, resentment, guilt, shame, etc.

Ask yourself, *What have the rocks done to my relationships with myself and others?*

Consider your past with your family and the life lessons you learned.

What rocks from your past are you bringing into the present?

What scripts or stories from the past have you written in your mind? These scripts are repeated thoughts that you've made a reality by repetition alone.

Do you hear old scripts playing over and over? What are they?

If you hear old scripts, are they self-damaging? How?

Have those scripts caused you to form beliefs, both negative and positive? What are they?

Reveal and write down something someone does that triggers you:

Ask yourself these two questions:

1. What am I afraid of if I reveal an old wound or secret?

2. What am I afraid to reveal?

8

Starting Over

"TIME'S UP!" *I heard. I gave myself a shake mentally, pulling my eyes away from the paper that lay on the table in front of me. The instructor I thought I was imagining was actually real and had just ended the exercise.*

I was sitting in a seminar, two years post-affair. Ron and I had committed that we would never stop growing and improving our marriage. I had just completed the first part of the "storyboard" activity that you'll find at the end of this chapter.

Now it was time for part two of the exercise, which was connecting the dots from my present-day life to how my past hurts had affected Ron and me in our marriage. At first, I wasn't sure I could continue—I was emotionally exhausted. But I also knew it was incredibly important for me to understand how my past directly connects to my "now."

I tried to regain my composure and listen to the instructions, but my head was still foggy. I was certain I had experienced a divine intervention.

The instructor told us to choose two or three hurtful things that had happened in our past and continued to negatively affect us. I looked at my sheet. On my storyboard I had written the word "commitment." As I stared at the paper, the word seemed to jump right out at me. I took my pen and proceeded to circle it: commitment. *It's a positive word for most people, especially when it comes to a significant relationship like the marriage covenant. That word was significant for me all right, but it was significant in a negative way. As I'll explain in detail later, the word "commitment" had an adverse effect on me as a child, thus coloring the way I viewed marriage.*

As a small group, we took turns sharing our storyboards with each other. When my turn arrived, I shared my word and instantly noticed the confusion on the faces of the other group members. However, as I began to explain my story, I could see understanding creep in.

I told them that when the word "commitment" showed up so clearly on my storyboard, I realized something. Three years before the infidelity occurred, my husband had tried to tell me something but I hadn't heard it because of the word "commitment."

Ron had written me a fourteen-page letter while I was away for a weekend. It's important to remember that this letter was written before the time computers were in every home providing a fast, easy way to save a document. This letter was handwritten; there was no duplicate.

I wish I could tell you what the whole letter said, but I can't. I can't because I never read past the second line, but I can share with you the first two lines. He wrote, "Babe, I love you, and I want our relationship to be better than it's ever been before. I am committed to this marriage . . ."

That was it. That's all I read before I began ripping the entire fourteen-page, handwritten letter into little pieces, making sure that no one would ever be able to put this thing back together again. Ron stood up—we had both been sitting on our bed in our home in White Rock, British Columbia. He looked at me in horror, saying, "What are you doing? Have you gone completely crazy?"

After I was done destroying his masterpiece of a letter, I calmly said, "Ron, I want a divorce." To say he was taken aback would be an understatement. He later told me that he thought he was in a nightmare.

"I don't know what planet you just came from," he replied, "but I'm going to leave now before I do or say something really stupid." He turned and walked away, getting only to the end of the hall before returning. "Wait," he said. "I believe you owe me enough respect to tell me what just happened. You couldn't even have read past the first paragraph?"

I responded in a matter-of-fact way. "Ron, I don't need a commitment to our marriage from you. All I ever wanted was your love and acceptance. If we are at the point where you need to be 'committed,' then I think I would rather we divorce now and save ourselves a lot of future pain."

He stood there in shock, and I could tell that my small group was also in shock as I shared the story with them. This behavior doesn't make sense to most people, unless you could see my story from a different perspective. I thank God that Ron was able to do so.

I continued, still with no emotion, "My mom was 'committed' to her marriage and kids because that was her duty as a *wife and mother; she was obligated to give up her life for us. She didn't want to be there, but her belief system was that when you make a commitment, you are obligated to fulfill it. Here's the thing though, Ron. When she was fighting with my dad, I would hear her say that she was committed to raising his children, but once the kids were out of the house, she would be gone too because he could take care of himself. My mom was only committed until a certain time. So tell me," I asked Ron coldly, "how long are you committed for? Until the kids are grown or until I'm old and can't start over? You just tell me until when!"*

The shock on his face was horrific, but what happened next caused my heart to melt. He came over to the bed and, even though I tried to resist, he wrapped his arms around me until I cried.

————◆————

This story really drives home that our belief system and perspective in life are ultimately formed by what we see, hear, and personally experience. The decisions we make today, based on our pasts, will affect our futures. For instance, my definition of commitment, which was based on my past experience, could have ended our marriage.

On that day when I asked for a divorce, Ron and I resolved the commitment issue, and much healing took place in the days to follow. Unfortunately, I discovered later through the storyboard exercise that many issues were left untouched. Those issues were in the fourteen-page letter I hadn't bothered to read.

We didn't deal with the fact that my husband felt neglected, unnurtured, and often alone emotionally. My penchant for drama consistently overshadowed his concerns, an issue he apparently addressed in the body of that letter. These unresolved issues played a huge part in the affair. I say this boldly at every speaking engagement, and I will say it here: "What you do not resolve will come back to haunt you!"

The work of resolving issues is worth it, although our society doesn't support this idea. Instead, it rationalizes these two false beliefs: "We all deserve to be happy" and "If your life together isn't working, then you should both move on." Finding happiness seems to be the goal nowadays rather than resolving conflict in a healthy manner. I was once told that if the pain of staying is greater than the pain of leaving, then leave. What horrible advice. The pain of two years gave me almost twenty years of joy! It was well worth the price, I'd say. Don't follow the trend of instant gratification; instead, seek ways to make your commitment to each other work.

I knew personally that the rebuild was going to take some work, but I needed more than just a decision that Ron would stay. I wanted our lives to matter, to really count for something. It was not just about being back on track for the healing of our broken hearts; I desired our ministry to be even more powerful than ever before. For me, in order for this to take place, our happiness, love, and restoration would depend on two conditions. I knew these two conditions needed to be met before Ron and I could be restored.

Condition Number One: "I Choose You"

He had to choose me. And his choice needed to be free and deliberate—of his own volition. My rejection issues were having a heyday. I felt like I was five years old again being told, "You should've never been born." I felt like the child no one missed when she wasn't around. I felt fat and ugly. I needed to know Ron wanted me. I didn't want a quick answer, and I didn't want to hear, "Let's give our marriage another shot, or let's at least try." In my mind, *trying* was an excuse for failure. I needed security.

I felt myself thinking like the women I had counseled. I remembered a young woman who once sat in my office crying, "Tina, if I forgive him and give him back my heart, then I risk it being broken again. How will I know for sure he won't do it again?" No one wants to risk pain; humans tend to avoid pain at any cost.

Now here I was, asking myself the same question as that young woman. I knew the risk and the cost, but still I wanted my husband's decision to be well thought out. I needed to know that he wanted our marriage, our family, our restoration. I knew loving feelings would follow the decision. But the decision needed to be made with a new vow of "until death do us part"! I knew it would take time for Ron to overcome his feelings for the other woman, but love and the decision to do the right thing could conquer this affair. I knew we could trust God on this; I had that assurance in my heart.

My fear was that Ron would stay with our children and me because it seemed easier than divorce, and that our marriage might fall apart again in the future.

Ron assured me that he had already decided to work on our marriage. Both Ron and my friend knew in their hearts that two wrongs don't make a right. They knew they belonged with their families.

Condition Number Two: A Different Kind of Forgiveness

The second condition would be harder for Ron to meet than the first. I needed him to forgive *himself*. I knew that our marriage would never work if unforgiveness and shame were allowed to be part of it. I was well aware that shame and unforgiveness are the devil's playground.

"Honey, I can choose you," Ron told me, "and I'm confident in the decision she and I both made to make our marriages work, but forgiving myself is going to take a lot more than a decision. It's going to take a miracle. I don't know how I will ever be able to forgive myself."

The Danger of Shame

Shame is a giant killer. It stops love and promotes self-loathing. I am speaking right now to both the betrayed and the betrayer. Shame will kill relationships every time, even your relationship with God. The big question is, how can you accept God's love, or anyone's love for that matter, when you can't even accept yourself? I knew I couldn't build a new marriage on top of that foundation.

If you, like Ron, feel unworthy or unlovable, or if you struggle with the desire to shut down or run away, you may be struggling with shame. We all make mistakes, and sometimes our actions fail to meet the standards that we have set for ourselves. Guilt is a healthy emotion to feel after we do something that we regret, something that falls below our standards, and it's healthy as long as it's temporary. Once repentance has occurred, guilt should subside.

Shame, on the other hand, is the unhealthy and harmful conviction that *you* are bad, and the debilitating weight of that thought makes it very hard to break toxic cycles in relationships. Shame might even have come to you from the actions or words of someone else, and it may be so deeply embedded in you that you don't even recognize it yet. Whatever the cause, shame will wreak havoc if left unresolved.

My mind was made up; I knew I couldn't live with someone who was wearing a cloak of shame. He would never be free, and we would never be able to progress if he didn't come to a place of genuine self-forgiveness. It would only be a matter of time before our marriage would come crashing down if he wasn't able to heal. It was then that I held out my hand and asked Ron for his wedding band.

He looked perplexed and in a bit of shock as he asked, "Why?"

My answer was simple: "Because it has lost its value. Babe, I want our marriage more than I've ever wanted anything before, but I want a *new* life with you—a life that is honest and healthy. I want to learn how to give you my whole heart and not be afraid of what might lie ahead of us. This is the scariest thing I've ever been through, but God has given me a glimpse of what He will do if we don't bow down to this pain. If you give me your ring, it will remind you that love requires forgiveness and that I don't think I can give you my heart fully until you forgive yourself."

In that moment, he slowly removed his ring and placed it in the palm of my hand.

Less than a month later, while we were on a much-needed

healing vacation in the Caribbean, he whispered in my ear, "Honey, I think I just forgave myself."

We cried together and held each other tight, and later that day I took him shopping for a new wedding band with a few tiny diamonds, signifying how we had just stepped out of the darkest place a marriage can be and into a bright new future.

Our eldest daughter, Jenny, wears that ring today. When her father passed away on December 25, 2013, I placed that ring on her finger because I thought it was the most precious gift her father would want her to have. The ring was a reminder of how forgiveness had benefited our family. Showing our children how to walk in forgiveness is the greatest gift we can give them. Forgiveness promises a new beginning and a bright future.

It's important to remember that forgiveness is not a magic pill or potion. My choice to forgive and live by the R3 principles didn't prevent everyone involved from suffering the consequences of the affair. The other woman and her husband; my husband and me; our children, families, supporters, friends, and peers: We *all* suffered. When betrayal occurs, no one escapes the pain. "But where sin increased, grace abounded all the more" (Romans 5:20). Thank God for His grace. While forgiveness doesn't guarantee a smooth and easy journey, it does have a reward of joy!

Creating Your Storyboard

At the beginning of this chapter, I shared a part of my storyboard experience to assure you once more that what you've seen, heard, and experienced in your past often affects your

current belief system and, in turn, affects how you interact in your relationships. My belief system told me that the
word "commitment" had a negative connotation, that com-
mitments had a beginning *and* an end, and it was my past
experience that caused me to threaten divorce that day with
Ron. Using the storyboard technique at the seminar showed
me how our pasts can influence our lives.

The storyboard also begged the question, "How well do
I know myself?" There is no one else quite like you. You are
a unique individual who has been developing over time and
through all your life experiences. Your special mix of hopes,
dreams, fears, quirks, habits, and personality is unmatched.
Have you taken the time to really know and understand
yourself? Do you ever find yourself wondering why you
behave a certain way?

Doing the storyboard exercise helps you focus internally
so you can increase self-awareness. It will help you understand what shapes your perspective, why you react as you
do, and why other people "just don't get it" when something
seems so clear to you. Understanding yourself will revolu-
tionize your behavior and relationships with others. Through
the storyboard exercise, you and your spouse will come to
understand yourselves individually, understand each other,
and learn how to grow more effectively together throughout
the rest of your lives.

God can and will take your pain and use it for good.
But it's important for you to recognize that sometimes your
reactions, because of your pain, contribute to the decisions
you make. Decisions based on lies from your past or on fear
won't help you. Please don't skip the storyboard exercise at

the end of this chapter, since it may be the most healing of all the exercises and the one that helps you connect your past to your present. It will help you view the stories of your past from a more mature and healthy viewpoint and rewrite your story today so you can live freely.

Storyboard Exercise

Everyone has a story full of ups and downs. God has already taken me on my "George Bailey" journey. What about you? If you'll only trust the process—and of course God's grace—you can end up on your own journey to healing and a wonderful life.

Read the following text slowly, pausing after each paragraph. Let yourself experience what may relate to you. You may want to jot down notes if that will help you to better process the questions in each paragraph.

Our past always influences our present—sometimes we just don't realize the extent of that influence. By revealing the story of our lives, we can discover which significant events, incidents, and transitions are profoundly influencing our present.

At this time, I would like you to get comfortable and relax. Begin to let your mind's eye reveal events that have taken place throughout your lifetime. I want you to think back in time. Start by picturing yourself as a young child. Do you have a photo of yourself as a small child? If so, focus on that picture. Focus on who you were when you were young.

Are you a happy or sad child? What are your concerns?

Are you worrying? If so, what are you worrying about? What does it feel like when you walk through the door of your home? Do you feel happy to be home? Is your father there? Is your mother there? Or do you feel like hiding from your parents? Are you afraid?

Do you have siblings? If so, how do you feel about them? Do you fight with them? Are you jealous of them? Are you the oldest child? Do you feel it's your job to make everyone feel okay? Or are you a middle child who feels invisible? Are you the youngest child in your family—the baby no one wants to listen to? Perhaps you are your parents' favorite, or maybe you are the black sheep of the family. Are you an only child? Do you feel jealous of other kids who have many siblings to play with? Do you feel alone?

What is it like when you go to school? Are you the popular kid? Are you the jock? Or are you the geek? Perhaps you are the last kid chosen when schoolyard games are played. Do you get teased? Are you a bully or are you bullied?

Picture yourself during your teen years. Are you rebellious or are you the good kid? Are you excelling in school or are you barely trying? How does your first romantic crush end? Do you end it? How do you treat the opposite sex? Does your extended family support you? Are they there for you, or are they hard on you? Are there deaths in your family? Divorce? Neglect? Abuse? Was someone you loved battling addiction?

Think about your life now. Are your plans working out? Are you accomplishing your goals? Marrying? Succeeding in your marriage? If you have children, do they say you are a good parent? Are you dealing with significant losses in your life? Illnesses? Lost careers? Lost dreams? Are you being punished or praised for your choices in life?

Each of these events and experiences had a shaping influence on you. Both the negative and the positive experiences have affected who you are today.

I suggest you now give God permission to walk you through all the crevices of your heart and mind.

Stop.

Breathe.

Pray.

The next step will be to create your storyboard.

Instructions for Creating Your Storyboard

To begin creating your storyboard, use two blank pages in a notebook turned to a horizontal position. Draw a horizontal line to divide the pages. Label the top half of the storyboard *Highs—Positive.* Label the bottom half of the storyboard *Lows—Negative.* Now begin to add bullet points above or below the line to indicate events in your life. If the incident was positive, place it above the line and add a few words to describe the event—for example, *chosen for the softball team.* If the event was negative, add a bullet point below the line and add a few words to describe the event—for example, *best friend moved.*

Use your storyboard to reveal the source of some of the hardness of your heart or even the vows you may have made and broken. Think about some of the highs and lows of your storyboard. Focus mostly on the younger years of your life, and see if you can connect how you might have brought some of the emotions from those experiences into your present relationships.

After you complete your storyboard, look at it again and circle two or three events that most negatively affected your life.

Tina's Sample Storyboard

Ask yourself:

Can I connect the dots between something that happened in my childhood with something that still affects my life today?

Do I feel more compassionate regarding my relationships now that I've learned from my storyboard?

Do I realize that everyone has his or her own story? By making this realization a part of my life, can I see my spouse and others through "eyes of compassion"?

Can I see myself through "eyes of compassion"?

The buried portion of a person's past will not stay buried if left unrevealed and unresolved. When the root has not been dealt with, emotions will continue to come up. Anything unresolved will surface more often than not in negative emotions and toxic thoughts.

Resolving the past did not come easily for me, and it may

not for you either. Nevertheless, my story is my gift for every person God calls me to meet and affect. If you are open to it, God can use your story in a similar way. At this moment, that idea probably seems absurd to you or even unwelcome. It surely did to me when my encouragers suggested that God would ultimately use our story to heal others. I didn't want to hear that while I was in the midst of my nightmare.

Yet buying this book is a step of faith on your part, and it suggests that you are open to rewriting your story. Know that your story isn't over. The next chapter has yet to be written. Continue moving forward by faith and put the work in. The past is the past. You have today and, God willing, many tomorrows. Use them to write the story you dream of.

9

Rules of Engagement

It was the end *of a beautiful day. For me, anytime there was sunshine in Vancouver, it was a good day. We were both getting ready for bed. For at least a year after the affair, bedtime was not pleasant for me. My desire to be intimate with my husband kept colliding with the terrible image in my mind of him and my best friend together. Their betrayal still felt like a fresh wound that created incredibly vivid nightmares—nightmares that caused me to wake up often, completely soaked in sweat and filled with nausea from the fear that tormented me.*

One particular night, as we prepared to turn out the lights, Ron kissed me good night and shared with me that he had some errands to run early the next morning. He told me that if I was still sleeping, he would not wake me. With that articulated and understood, we both drifted off to sleep. Morning came, and I heard Ron get up. I heard the shower running, but by the time Ron came back into the bedroom I had drifted off again. He bent over me and gave me a gentle kiss. "Love you, Babe," he said. "I'll see you later."

Still in a stupor, I opened my eyes, kissed him back, and said, "I love you, too. Have a good day." I rolled over and closed my eyes once more, hoping to catch another hour of rest before starting my day.

I wish I could tell you what exactly happened next, but it's still a blur to me. I only know that when I woke up a couple of hours later, around 8 a.m., a dark cloak of sadness had settled over me. I got up and padded over to the bathroom. This feeling was not unusual at this stage of our renewal, but what followed next was totally out of the ordinary. As I walked out of the bathroom, I was hit with an unexpected rush of anger. It washed over me like a tidal wave. I found myself in the walk-in closet, pulling out all of Ron's clothes, crying and yelling, "I can't do this! God, I thought I could be strong, but I'm not!"

I felt as if my whole body was in some bizarre, remote-controlled state! It was exactly how I imagined having an out-of-body experience would feel. Just two hours earlier, I had kissed the man these clothes belonged to and said, "I love you. Have a good day." Now here I was throwing every shirt and every pair of pants and shoes from the closet. By the time I was finished, there was not one piece of Ron left in that closet.

I was exhausted, and it was only 10 a.m. My heart was pounding, the tears were flowing, and the devil had me up against the ropes. Standing in that empty closet, I felt completely defeated. I couldn't think straight, and I most definitely was not interested in hearing God's voice right then. I was angry and felt I had earned this meltdown. I didn't want to cry anymore after I made love with my husband. I didn't want to have those paralyzing nightmares that haunted my sleep night after night. But mostly, I just couldn't handle feeling so alone in my pain.

Don't think it hadn't occurred to me on more than one occasion that maybe I was the issue. I was cloaked in pain day and night. I prayed relentlessly for a break, a respite from the deep grief, but for whatever reason, God remained silent. But the devil did not. He pounced on anything that would hurt, scare, or anger me.

Be forewarned that when we are down, the enemy will strike, and he will strike to kill. I knew this to be true, even as I sat in that half-empty closet after hurling Ron's clothes into the hall, because on top of everything else I had faced, I had recently lost my dad to cancer. Believe me when I say that the devil will seek to overload an already overloaded soul.

My closet floor felt like a pit of nothingness. I have no idea how long I sat there. It seemed like days, but when I heard my bedroom door open, the reality of what I had done hit me head-on. I'd been in a trance!

It's important to see how this enemy-induced trance can fool both the betrayer and the betrayed. I didn't betray my husband, but his sin was now inspiring my sin.

The trance lifted when the bedroom door opened. I was back in my right mind, and I would have to face the consequences of my actions. I could hear Ron's steps echoing on our wooden floor and his voice calling out, "Honey? Babe, are you in here?" And then, in amazement, "Honey! Babe!"

As Ron came around the corner into the hallway, the first

thing he saw was the mountain of clothes that stood between him and me. At first, it didn't dawn on him that all of those things were his.

"Whoa, Babe!" he said. "Are you on a major cleaning rampage?"

Then he saw me on the floor, my face stained with tears. It became clear that I was not cleaning out the closet, but cleaning him out of my life.

"What the heck is going on?" he said in total disbelief. "What are you doing?"

I gazed up at him, overcome with sorrow. Yet that emotion quickly changed to rage as I screamed, "I can't do this! You need to leave. I can't do this pain day in and day out. It's not letting up." I was back in the trance, only now it had turned from intense sadness to extreme anger.

Ron tried to come closer, gently navigating his way over, around, and through the pile of his life that earlier had been left neatly hanging or folded or placed in an orderly manner in the closet we shared. As he approached, I told him to get out and, in less than subtle terms, expressed that I wanted to exercise my right to divorce him. All I can say is thank God for school because my children never witnessed any of these "crazy times."

Ron wouldn't leave, so I started yelling for him to get out. The enemy is fierce and cunning, and ready to magnify any negative emotion, which is why God so specifically tells us in His Word to guard our hearts.

Turning away, I heard the bedroom door slam and then the front door slam. That's when fear hit me—hard. I retreated to the fetal position and curled up on that floor, knowing I had crossed the point of no return. He was gone. What had I done?

Why didn't he hold me, even if I told him not to touch me? That's what he had always done before; surely he knew by now not to ignore me when I got like this. Why didn't he stay?

I'm not sure how much time passed. It felt like hours, but it was probably only a minute or two. As I lay there, wishing I could die, I felt two strong arms circle around me, followed by Ron's entire body enveloping my whole being. It was as though he could somehow hold me from the inside out. My man had come back, and he held me until I calmed down. Lying there on the floor, we cried together and held each other like our very lives depended on us staying connected. We made love. I cried again.

———— • ————

After the trance had broken and I had finally gotten off that roller coaster of emotions, Ron and I realized that we needed to have some boundaries, some "rules to live by." In order to handle future issues in a healthy manner, we needed some practical tools. We had to learn to "fight healthy" as we moved toward healing in our marriage, and we had to find new ways to interact with each other. I call what we set in motion our "rules of engagement."

Rule #1: Don't keep secrets. Secrets keep you sick. We knew that if we were going to move forward, we would have to build on a foundation of truth and honesty. We would have to be open and vulnerable with each other, even in the seemingly insignificant things.

Rule #2: Bless each other. We decided to say a prayer each day thanking God for each other. Every day, pray aloud with your spouse, thanking God for the gift your spouse is to you. We knew that this was a "must" if we wanted to have a healthy marriage. There is power in the words we speak over each other.

Rule #3: Share all passwords and accounts. We would share total and complete access to each other's accounts, including our social media, e-mail, and phones. I knew all of Ron's passwords and he knew mine. We shared all accounts and credentials so neither was tempted. We knew there was safety in being accountable to each other in this way.

Rule #4: Practice full disclosure. We made a commitment to no half-truths or omitted details. The only exception was if we both agreed on not wanting to know everything, especially concerning the details of the affair. Note: If you are the betrayer, fully answer questions that are asked of you. If you are the betrayed, be honest about how much you want to know.

Rule #5: Do not withhold physical intimacy. The decision to restore your marriage simply cannot be taken seriously without this bond. Intimacy needs to be restored as soon as possible, even if your tears blind you and soak the bed linens before, during, or after. More times than not, tears *did* soak my sheets and pillow. Even so, the healing we experienced more than made up for the waterfall that would cascade down my cheeks each time. Sex is sacred in marriage, which explains why there is so much pain involved in a betrayal. Physical intimacy makes us one, and when that bond is broken our entire being feels it. The Bible speaks of the importance of this special bond between a husband and a wife: "Do not deprive one another, except perhaps by agreement for a limited time, that you may devote yourselves to prayer; but then come together again, so that Satan may not tempt you because of your lack of self-control" (1 Corinthians 7:5).

Make no mistake: This Scripture is talking about sex. I realize that at this time, these words may be the last ones you care to hear. But trust me: This verse will never be more applicable and will never hold more healing power for you than right now. So pray as much as you both need to, but don't let Satan mess with you anymore by using sex as a weapon.

Rule #6: Get sound counsel. It has been said that "no man is an island" and that "wisdom is found in the multitude of counselors," and this is so true. Our ministry, Relationship Lifeline, and others like it exist in order for hurting couples to receive wisdom and guidance as they move toward a healthy marriage. Wise advice can come from your pastors, church leaders, close friends, counselors, and other couples who have overcome in this area. Have in place a support system on your road to recovery and restoration. Don't try to do this alone.

Rule #7: Surround yourself with people who want your marriage to succeed. If we had listened to the negative advice of those who believed Ron and I should divorce, we would have missed out on twenty more years together, as well as on seeing countless other marriages restored through our testimony. Instead, we made a decision that we would surround ourselves with those who believed in our marriage covenant and were willing to stand in agreement with us.

Rule #8: Set boundaries to protect both of you. Be on guard against those insecurities from your past that may pop up again, especially when you are at your weakest point. We both had to accept that there would be bad days. We also had to expect them, but more importantly, we needed to be aware that when our trancelike episodes happened—or, as I called them, "my crazy"—we needed boundaries and a clear plan that we could both follow, something that mapped out what we needed from each other.

Rule #9: Identify why you feel the way you do. Ron learned something that "closet" day that was vital to the restoration of our marriage. He realized that no matter what I said or did, he needed to be there for me. Leaving me in a frantic, scared state of mind would not create in me a sense of safety but would instead reinforce my deep-seated, lifelong fear of abandonment—a fear that charged to the top of the list of issues I was facing during this time. This fear came from my belief system. Long before that day, I had learned that when things get tough, people run. Personally, my weakest link is the feeling of *rejection*, and the nightmare I woke up from on that particular morning triggered an explosion of emotion. Fear of abandonment gets me every time. It takes me to the darkest places of my innermost being and makes me do things I don't want to do, and that I know are wrong. So the rule we set in place that day was that when I did "crazy," Ron couldn't walk out and abandon me no matter what I said. Of course, your trigger(s) will be different, so you and your partner will need to develop your own rule(s) that serve to protect you both when old patterns rear their ugly heads.

Rule #10: If you are going to be late, call! If you don't call your spouse and alleviate worry, you can leave an opening for Satan. Doubt is powerful, causing people to stumble. It's easy to take this foothold away from the enemy, so make this your habit.

As much as we tended to act like children and wanted to rebel against the rules, we also were smart enough to realize we needed them desperately. Without them, we would once again leave ourselves open to the enemy's devices, and that was simply not acceptable. The process was difficult and at times seemed so legalistic, but I thank God that He impressed upon us the need for these ground rules.

We also had confidence that God would be with us in this process. He is a good God. He will not leave you. You can trust Him to be there every step of the way. Psalm 27:10 says, "For my father and my mother have forsaken me, but the LORD will take me in."

10

Moving On

R2: Rewrite is the next step to healing the pain of your past. The amazing thing about *revealing* your rocks is that it allows you to *rewrite* the toxic emotions raised by each rock. You don't have to live as a prisoner in bondage to toxic patterns. You can rewrite your story!

To rewrite your script, you'll need to see the event you revealed from a different mental, emotional, and spiritual perspective. You'll need to get a bird's-eye view of what you revealed in order to consider your story from a new, healthier viewpoint. Think of seeing your past from an altitude of 10,000 feet instead of just a few inches in front of your face.

Your Past Is the Key to Rewriting Your Future

The past can't be changed, so you may ask: How do I rewrite my story? Do I just tell another story? Do I lie about my story and say it never happened, or that it wasn't really that bad? No. But there is a way of rewriting your story so it no longer imprisons you. Although your narrative cannot be changed, it can become something brand-new! Second Corinthians 5:17 says, "Therefore, if anyone is in Christ, he is a new creation. The old has passed away; behold, the new has come."

If you are a believer, this Scripture is a reality in your life. You have been transformed spiritually, but a transformation also needs to take place in your mind and your emotions. How you see things—your perspective—also needs to change. Without a transformation in your mind and emotions, you are settling for less than God intends for you to have. In Romans 12:2, Paul says to "be transformed by the renewal of your mind, that by testing you may discern what is the will of God, what is good and acceptable and perfect." Let God transform you into a new person by changing the way you think.

Through transformation not only of your mind but also your spirit and emotions, you have the opportunity to break generational cycles of dysfunction. You can make a difference not only in your own life but also in the lives of the next generation.

So how do you rewrite your story? The answer is to do it the way Jesus did: with compassion. Even while Jesus was being crucified He said, "Father, forgive them." He was asking His Father not only to forgive the people who stood beneath the cross but also to forgive us today.

The events in your story can only be rewritten when you allow the hardness of your heart to be removed through the process of forgiveness. As you begin to view your story through the eyes of compassion, it will start to rewrite itself because the rewriting process is made available when you choose to forgive. As you begin the process of changing (rewriting) your story with a heart of compassion, then peace and grace will drive the narrative.

How do you gain this heart of compassion, especially for someone who abused and hurt you? Does having compassion for someone mean that you're also justifying what that person did to you? Does it mean that what they did was okay? No, but compassion *does* ask you to look at what led to the injustice.

You can find compassion when you look from a new perspective at the person who needs your forgiveness. Consider the person's history. What events took place in this person's life that may have led him or her to hurt you? Even if you don't know that person's history, think about what might have happened in the past that could have affected him or her. If you need to forgive an abusive parent, think about that parent's childhood. Picture your parent or the person you need to forgive as a child. Do you think it was this person's goal to grow up and hurt you? Definitely not. Can you feel *some* compassion for this person? If so, you are on your way to experiencing a transformation of your mind and emotions.

Forgiveness is not about changing the past or excusing the offense. It's about letting go of the toxic emotions and thoughts that you carry so the offender no longer has power over your life. Forgiveness means freedom for you!

When you can think back about the hurt or the person who hurt you without resentment or pain, then you'll be viewing that person through eyes of compassion.

Matthew 7:2 says, "For in the way you judge, you will be judged" (NASB). Don't we all want God to judge us with mercy and compassion? Jesus died for the person who hurt you. Holding bitterness, unforgiveness, or resentment in your mind and emotions means that you are acting as that person's judge.

The Three Steps of the Rewrite Process

There are three steps in the rewrite process. First, *decide* that you want to rewrite the hurts and pains of your past into something much better and healthier. We are creatures of free will; therefore, nothing can begin unless we choose to initiate it. Your choice is the cornerstone of change.

The second step in rewriting your script is viewing others, especially those who have wronged you, with compassion. Realize that everyone carries painful baggage and you have no idea what is in someone else's heart.

Thirdly, you must walk in forgiveness. Carrying the weight of hatred, resentment, anger, or anything else that does not serve up a positive endgame is not going to help you rewrite your script; in fact, unforgiveness will hinder the process. When you release others, you open the door to a new perspective. Forgiveness will give you a new way to see your past, both the good and bad, as well as a new way to see other people's pasts, the good and bad. It will be a fresh start, an opportunity to move forward.

Now is a good time to:

Stop.

Breathe.

Pray.

Give God permission to help you look at those who have hurt you and see them differently. Ask Him to help you see through eyes of compassion.

Rewrite Exercise: Renaming Your Rocks

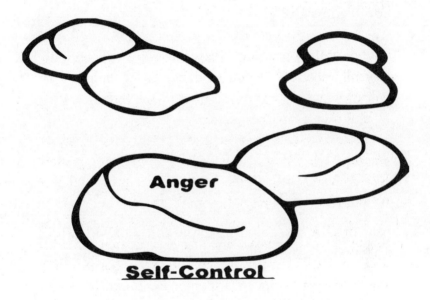

Rename the rocks you named in the reveal exercise. For each rock, write one word that can replace the toxic emotion. For example, we could replace "anger" with "self-control" or "peace," "bitterness" with "forgiveness," "judgmental" with "tolerant" or "nonjudgmental," "procrastination" with "persistence," and "confronting" with "agreeable" or "peaceable."

Words have the power of life and death. Proverbs 18:21 paraphrased in *The Message* says, "Words kill, words give life; they're either poison or fruit—you choose." Words have the power to heal and the power to destroy. Choose *life* by choosing words that build up rather than tear down, words that bring unity rather than division. The power is in your tongue!

Forgiveness Exercise

List two or three people who have hurt you—the ones you may still feel bitter, resentful, and unforgiving toward.

From that list, select one person who hurt you. Write what that person did, how it made you feel, and how it affects you today.

Write something about that person's history that might have led him or her to hurt you. If you don't know anything about the person's history, think about what might have happened to the person who hurt you.

Repeat this exercise for each person on your list who hurt you.

Finally, write a short letter to each person you have chosen to forgive. Date your letter and start with, "I choose to forgive you for…" End the letter with, "I choose to let go of the pain you have caused me by looking at you through eyes of compassion. I allow God's healing power of transformation to begin a renewal process in my life."

These letters aren't meant to be sent to anyone; they're meant to help you release your emotions onto paper. The process of letting go through writing is powerful.

The Amazing Effect of Forgiveness

I want to share a true story with you because it is an amazing example of the dramatic, physical change that forgiveness can have on a person.

Several years ago, a husband and wife attended one of our seminar weekends. You could tell that the husband had been forced to come. His warning to his wife was, "If they even *mention* God in this seminar, I'm out of there!" He quickly reconsidered his statement after learning that our money-back guarantee was based on participation in the entire weekend. Armed with this information, he decided that he would "grin and bear it" and then ask for his money back once the weekend was over.

When we addressed the forgiveness process on day three, his hackles went up. He was immediately defensive. This alcoholic biker dude was not going to forgive that blankety-blank father of his—no way, no how!

My husband looked at the man, and with the calmest yet sternest voice you've ever heard, said, "Sir, how has this anger and booze been working in your marriage?"

That question was enough to throw this guy completely off his game, but he realized that Ron, who was running the seminar, demanded an answer. In the end, Ron succeeded in leading this angry, defensive, hurt man to forgiveness.

One month later this biker dude and his wife traveled from Arizona, where they lived, to our next four-day seminar to help out as volunteers. Ron and I didn't recognize the man, but we knew it *had* to be him since he was with his wife.

"No worries," the man said with a laugh. "I can tell by the look on your faces that you don't recognize me. Neither did my mother when I went to meet her for lunch last week!" He told us that prior to their flight from Phoenix to Orange County, he couldn't even get through security until a special agent did a facial recognition test. His face didn't match the face on his driver's license, so security questioned his identity.

Never doubt the power of forgiveness!

11

Protecting Your Kids

FOR A WHILE, *every day seemed to bring its own unique storm in those early weeks after the end of the affair. Ron and I needed to make many decisions if we were going to truly rewrite our story, and those decisions involved not only our marriage but also our children's lives. Our kids were fifteen and eleven at the time—rough years on a good day, even without the emotional trauma they had been forced to endure.*

Ron and I had to decide what to tell them, how much to tell them, and when to tell them. Talk about a dilemma. We waited a couple of weeks before we said anything, all the while knowing that our kids recognized the sad energy trapped inside our once happy home. The sudden end of our close friendship with the other woman's family didn't help either.

I can only imagine how not knowing what was happening to their mom and dad must have hurt them. It still breaks my heart to think of how they must have been feeling during that time.

Sometimes the right choice isn't always clear. Do we tell our children the whole truth? Or do we consider what is age appropriate and share only that? The counsel we received was to tell our fifteen-year-old daughter more detail of her father's affair and tell our son that sometimes adults do really bad things, and because of that, friendships end badly. Either way, we had to deliver bad news that we knew would hurt our kids. The only question now was how much to share with them. We chose the lesser of two evils in our minds and shared what we felt was age appropriate.

I remain grateful to this day for the good counsel we received at that time from some amazing people. Their wise advice helped our family navigate the storm and come through the other side together.

———— •◦• ————

Trying to recover from infidelity in a marriage is very taxing for the betrayed *and* the betrayer. Because of this, it can be easy to forget that there are often others who may be affected by an affair. Let me take a moment to speak about the issue of raising healthy kids in the midst of the chaos because, let's face it, there are days when you may "lose it" emotionally. If you have children, it's imperative that your kids are out of the house when you have your fully expected meltdowns. If your children are home, you'll need to leave the house. Your trauma can and will affect your children. The degree to which it does is up to you.

This truth became emphatically clear to me when I was giving birth to my son, Joshua. At the end of my labor, my precious little boy decided he wanted to make his grand entrance positioned head up, looking at the ceiling instead of the floor. As he did his acrobatic, full-body twist, I let out a loud, bloodcurdling scream.

The doctors and nurses had to move quickly. My son's maneuver was dangerous for him *and* for me. They rushed me from the labor room to the operating room while Ron scrambled to keep up, all the while trying to comfort me. I wasn't having any of it; I continued screaming so loudly, and for so long, that Ron said later that he thought something had taken over my body! Well, it had. It was a nine-pound baby!

My screaming seemed to ease the pain, so I continued my tirade for the entire gurney ride. I was told later about the chaos that was happening around me, but at the time I was too busy being in agony to care much about what anyone else was doing. But when they had to switch me from my bed to an operating table, a nurse suggested in a firm voice that I stop screaming and cooperate with them.

But screaming helped, and I was not about to stop until the pain did. That nurse wasn't going to let me ignore her, however. All of a sudden, she slapped me across the face with all her might! I'm certain the sound of her open palm hitting my cheek echoed throughout the entire floor.

My nurse *instantly* had my full and unwavering attention. She became the only thing I could hear, and I will never forget what she said: "Tina, you're putting the baby in trauma. You need to calm yourself down and *breathe*. You need to help us move you to the operating table."

Those are the words she used, but what *I* heard was that my baby was in grave danger! That was all it took for me to stop thinking about my own pain and start focusing on my precious baby's well-being.

Where's Your Focus?

Do you understand my story? Is it speaking to you? Are you focusing only on your own pain right now? You have a choice to make, just as I did as I lay on that gurney.

Eventually, I did calm down, and you need to as well. I had my son by natural birth and everything turned out okay, thank God. But I could have lost him that day, and that thought has never left me. If that group of amazingly talented doctors and nurses hadn't worked as quickly and efficiently as they did, and if I had continued fighting the process because of my pain, the outcome could have been tragically different.

Because of my lack of self-control, I was slowing the birthing process. I was stopping the transition. I was becoming a part of the problem. When the baby flipped, the cord wrapped around his tiny little neck. He had stopped breathing. I thank God for the boldness of that nurse. If she had not slapped me silly, it's very probable that I would not have a son.

Let me be that nurse today for you. Let me be the person who gives you a loving but massive, metaphorical slap across the face! At some point, an unexpected jolt is what we need to get us moving forward and out of our funk.

Now that I've given you that slap, I'm asking you to

breathe . . . take a few deep, purifying, life-giving breaths. Now shake it off. You need to get this pain out of the way and protect the children you have nurtured and cared for.

Protect the Kids from Your Pain

Whether you're the one who has been hurt or the one who committed adultery, your job is to protect your children. They are victims, and they do not deserve to be forcibly attached to your pain.

Your children simply can't process what they are witnessing. Think of how difficult this situation is for you to process mentally and emotionally. Now put yourself in the body of your five-year-old, eight-year-old, or teenager, and realize that what you decide to do right now can affect them as adults.

There is no greater selfishness than to knowingly harm a child emotionally or physically. So have your meltdown, yell, scream, kick, and throw things (not at someone), but do it while your kids are safely elsewhere, perhaps at a relative's or friend's house, or while they are at school.

If you are anything like me, you can feel when your emotions are going to overpower you. When you feel your emotions begin to build, be proactive and think of your kids first. Out-of-control behavior witnessed by a child can do long-term damage, so shelter them from it.

Even if you have been betrayed, the other person is still your child's mom or dad, so don't start calling your spouse names. To protect your children, soften some of that rage you may be feeling. You can do that when you own *your part* of this catastrophic mess.

Be a Role Model

When my daughter, Jenny, was struggling to forgive her dad, she once said to me, "Mom, I'm not like you. I don't think I will ever be able to forgive Dad. And Mom, how could you forgive *her*?"

That day I knew I had to set an example. I didn't want to put my children in the place of protecting me from the awful thing their dad and our friend had done.

Jenny eventually did forgive, but not until she witnessed the love her father and I had for each other and what the power of forgiveness had done in our home. Children learn forgiveness by how we live our lives after we have been wronged. This is where they learn not to "repay evil for evil" (1 Peter 3:9). We shared our testimony with hundreds of people on many stages, and Jenny had heard her father express many times that his wife never held his sin against him after she forgave him. She heard her dad share that this is how he was eventually able to forgive himself.

Just as Jenny saw her dad through my eyes, I had learned to see Ron through God's eyes. And seeing what God sees is the greatest gift I can give to anyone reading this book. Our eyes see through hurt, anger, bitterness, rejection, or self-pity. But I thank God that He granted me the miracle of seeing Ron, my best friend, and this entire situation through His eyes. You, too, can ask God to open your eyes today. God promises to give you eyes to see if only you will ask.

Children Don't Get Divorced

I do what I am called to do, as a public speaker and the director and facilitator of Relationship Lifeline, because I believe that children deserve to grow up in an environment with two healthy parents.

Even if the parents eventually decide that divorce is their only option, any child involved deserves to be raised by a healthy mom and a healthy dad. That means healing is vital if you want to do what's best for your children.

If you do choose divorce, just remember that while you may have a chance to "start over," your kids, more times than not, are not afforded that same option. And you might be surprised to know that the vow you once made—"till death us do part"—doesn't magically disappear once the divorce is finalized. After the divorce, your kids remain the victims of adult choices.

Divorce means shared custody, two houses, possibly stepparents to deal with, and adjustments that your children have to make. Let's look ahead a bit and see what the future holds for children of divorce. What will birthdays, holidays, graduations, baptisms, and school events look like? Now let's look even further ahead. How are children of divorce affected when they become engaged, get married, and have children? How are you affected? If you want to be a part of your kids' lives, you will inevitably have to deal with your ex-spouse. There's no getting around it.

I can hear you say, "We'll have alternate holidays." So who decides what the schedule is? Once your children are adults, they will. You will constantly be putting them in awkward and awful positions to sort out your failed marriage long after your marriage fails. So you see, divorce doesn't really end anything. It just makes things infinitely more complicated.

Since you can't escape graduations, weddings, births of grandchildren, etc., the burden is on *you* to become your best self. You really have no choice but to make your emotional, physical, and spiritual renewing an important part of your healing and growth, whether you reconcile or divorce.

Your children should never suffer tension or anxiety over the thought of their parents being together. Your divorce or negative opinion of the other spouse (their mom or dad, remember) is not your children's cross to bear. Your divorce was not their decision.

Please hear me when I say that you can't let your healing be optional, no matter the outcome of your marriage relationship. You can talk about healing all day long and twice on Sunday, but until you take action, that's all it will be: *talk*. Actions *do* speak louder than words, so stop talking, arguing, and debating, and start revealing, rewriting, and renewing your story today.

In spite of everything that happened between my husband and the other woman, I admired how she protected her children throughout the ordeal. To this day, even though her marriage ended and her children are now adults, she encourages them to have a relationship with their dad. She put their kids first, and that says a lot about her character and commitment to their mental and emotional health.

Even during the hardest, ugliest times, she kept their home as emotionally safe as possible. No matter what she had to endure, her heart for her children came above her feelings for herself or her marriage. She had messed up, and that was bad enough. She was determined that her children would not become collateral damage to her moral failure. No matter the circumstance, parents are called to protect their kids.

The Impact on Kids

As you work to protect your kids, it might be helpful for you to hear how my children were affected by that traumatic time in our lives. Jenny and Joshua share some of their thoughts in the following section.

Jenny

Growing up, I always knew I had a special dad. He did everything with us. He played with us, tickled us, and let us crawl into bed with him every Saturday morning. He taught us how to ski and dirt bike and play hockey. He told us we were special. He was proud of us.

He even took me on daddy-daughter dates. I remember our first one. I got all dressed up, and he "picked me up" at the front door. He even opened the car door for me. We went to an Italian restaurant and ordered escargot, the fanciest thing on the menu. He asked me about school and my friends. I'll never forget how special I felt.

He bought me an "Archie" comic every time we went to the grocery store. Every single day he told me I was beautiful. He listened, and he cared. My dad was my safety growing up. He was *there*. I knew that not everyone had that stability. Even as a young girl, I remember most of my friends at school either didn't have a father or didn't have a good one. They wanted to come to my house all the time because I did.

My dad protected us, and I adored him. I was Daddy's little girl, and I knew he adored me, too.

And then suddenly I had to change schools again.

"Why?" I asked my parents. "I just started making friends at this school! I don't understand. Why is this happening?"

I don't remember exactly what my parents told me that day; I just remember feeling unimportant, like my life didn't matter. My school didn't matter. My opinion didn't matter. *I* didn't matter.

"There were some feelings between your dad and another woman," is what they told me. At least that was the gist of it. Since I was fourteen, it was all I needed to know.

Five years would pass before my mom explained everything. Once she did, the truth deeply affected me. We were sitting in my car, pulled over less than a block away from our home, as she told me why she had uprooted our family and turned our lives upside down. We were on our way home from a women's conference where we had seen *her* (the other woman). It was the first time we had seen her in five years.

I was in shock. I think I knew at some level about the affair, but I didn't really *know*. Once the truth was confirmed, I wondered if my dad's love for me had all been a lie. I concluded that every hug, every "I love you," every tuck-in, story, and back scratch must have been an act. If he had been willing to risk our special bond for the other woman, his love for me couldn't have been true in the first place. How could someone who loved us so much ever do that?

"Leave him." That's right. That was my advice to my own

mother. "Why would you stay? He made a total fool of you . . . of us."

Because of the affair, I developed a new belief system. These thoughts became my truth:

- All men will hurt you.
- If the perfect husband (and father) can do this, then what chance do I have of finding someone who won't?
- I will never let a man humiliate me like that.
- Don't get close enough for them to hurt you.
- Don't trust.
- Don't love.
- Use them before they use you.
- Stick to short, uncommitted relationships. That way, no one gets hurt.
- Find a jerk so you won't be surprised when he treats you badly. You won't get attached. You'll see it coming.

After that day, my heart began to harden. I was so angry with my dad. I felt rejected. In my mind, his infidelity meant he was willing to risk never seeing me again. What he did was the most selfish thing I could fathom. I lost all respect for my father and couldn't believe a word he said. I'm not saying my response was fair; it's just how I felt.

Our relationship fell apart. I began to push my dad away. I became rude and snarky. I acted disrespectfully to him in public and in private. How dare he ask me where I was going or what time I'd be home? Even if I was going out with boys (which I usually was), I could never do anything as wrong as what he had done. After all, I wasn't married. I wasn't cheating. He had lost all right to tell me what to do.

During this time, I ended many potentially great relationships because I was too scared to be hurt again.

Years later, by the grace of God, my dad and I began to rebuild our relationship. We talked and worked at it, and we healed. My heart experienced true forgiveness. We renewed our relationship, which became better than it ever was before. Even so, we lost many years.

I cannot tell you how thankful I am that my mom, whom I once judged for allowing my dad to stay, decided to fight for her marriage. I'm proud of both of my parents for persevering, healing, and renewing their relationship. I know it wasn't easy and there were times when they both wanted to quit. But my life would have been different if they hadn't stayed the course.

If they hadn't fought for their marriage, I know I wouldn't have started Whole Way House, an organization that helps men transition out of homelessness. Whole Way House is a legacy of my parents' instruction about compassion and their modeling it for us.

I know Relationship Lifeline would not be operating today if my parents had ended their marriage. Thousands of people's lives would not be changed and influenced by my parents' teaching. Families would not be saved from divorce and trauma.

And I probably wouldn't have been my dad's primary caregiver as cancer spread throughout his body. I would not have spent every day and night with him, timing his medications and learning how to give injections and how to increase the dosage based on his pain levels. I would not have been able to bathe his bony body, or change his sweat-soaked sheets, or wipe his brow after he vomited. I wouldn't have been there to rub his feet, scratch his back, and make him food that he could keep down. I wouldn't have been there to hear him share his intimate thoughts and dreams with me, to hold his hand, and to just lie there with him when he was in pain.

Most of all, I wouldn't have been there with him when he could no longer speak, when he moaned to get my attention. And when I asked if he wanted me to get the rest of the family, he grabbed my arm so strongly that I knew his answer was yes. So we all prayed with him, held him, and were there with him as he took his last breaths. I know that experience wouldn't have happened if my parents hadn't decided to fight for their marriage. I will be forever thankful to them, if only for that one hour at my dad's deathbed when we were all together. That moment is priceless, and I will cherish it for the rest of my life.

My dad's legacy lives on today and will continue to live on for generations to come because of the decision my parents made, a decision to look beyond themselves and see what God could do with their marriage and family.

Joshua

I was eleven years old, and we had just returned from spending the Christmas holidays at my grandma's house in Trail. I was ready to get back to school because our Christmas hadn't been full of good tidings, joy, or peace. It hadn't been full of the usual steaming borscht and homemade goodies made by my grandma, or the snowball fights, skiing, and tobogganing.

Instead, the season had been heartbreaking. My grandma was seriously ill, and we knew she probably wouldn't make it through Christmas. During our stay we spent countless hours in Grandma's room praying, singing, and crying. Grandma was always thinking of others first, and it seemed she was doing that even at the end of her life. She managed to hold on through the holiday week, finally passing away on the day after Christmas.

After we returned to Vancouver, I was glad to be with my school friends. Leaving all the sadness of the holidays behind felt good, but I noticed that my mom and dad were still acting differently when they were together. I figured it was just because Dad was having a hard time with Grandma's passing.

One morning as I was getting ready for school, I heard my mom crying in the bedroom. Then I heard yelling, followed by my dad saying what I thought was, "Maybe I should leave." Dad usually drove me to school, but this particular morning Mom drove me. Her eyes were red, so I knew she had been crying. "Mom," I said in a matter-of-fact way, "you can't get a divorce!"

Shocked by my statement, Mom simply asked, "Why not?"

"Because at your seminars, you help people not get divorces!"

She started crying and then assured me that she and Dad were not getting a divorce. I was relieved to hear that news. A few of my friends' parents were divorced, and I knew they hated it.

But my circumstances were about to change anyway. It wasn't long before my parents told my sister and me that we needed to move to Sacramento for business reasons. They were training a couple there to run the marriage seminars, they explained, and it would be easier to live there for a while.

I had just switched schools that year so I could be with my best friend, and now I had to move! My sister was given the option of homeschooling with our cousins in Trail, so that's what she did. But I didn't have an option. I was moving to Sacramento, and that was that.

Sacramento had been a fun place when we traveled there with Mom and Dad for their seminars, but I'd never had any interest in living there. Yet now I was being forced to do just that. I missed my home, my friends, and my bedroom.

In our tiny new place, my bedroom was the living room. And my new school was a nightmare. The teachers humiliated me, and homework lasted for hours each night. The Canadian and US curriculums were worlds apart. I was used to metric math and certainly didn't know US history. Everything was different and seemed harder for me.

My parents were still acting weirdly, and the change just didn't make sense. My mom cried a lot. She tried to hide it, but I still knew. She seemed always to be in her room.

We spent five months there before we went home. Unfortunately, we were returning because my mom's dad was very sick. He had cancer and was given at most only a few months to live. So we packed up the few belongings we had and headed back to Canada. It didn't seem like much time had passed since my dad's mom had passed, and now my mom's dad was dying. My mom took her dad's death especially hard and, for several months, rarely came out of her room.

I did my best to convince myself that the strangeness I saw between my mom and dad was due to the two deaths happening so closely together. But somehow I knew there was another reason for the sadness in our house. I would hear bits and pieces, fragmented sound bites that made me aware of this fact. I would ask my sister about this on occasion, because I figured she might know something I didn't. Why had our parents' closest friends stopped coming over? And why couldn't we see their kids anymore?

She would just say, "You have to ask Mom and Dad."

No one told me the truth for a long time. Yet after a little while, Mom and Dad seemed even happier than before. I eventually forgot about that strange time.

One Friday afternoon, I came home early from school. Mom must not have heard me as I ran up the stairs. Her bedroom door was open, and she was in there with a friend. I was about to walk in when I overheard Mom say that it had been a rough couple of years after Ron's affair.

To say I was shocked would be a colossal understatement. Mom continued saying that she was so happy that they had stayed together. She kept talking, having no idea I was right outside the door listening to every word. She expressed how it was a double whammy of betrayal because the affair had been with her best friend. She was trying to tell the friend in the room about how God's love covered all of our wrongs.

The first thing I did was head straight to my sister and demand to know whatever she knew. I even asked her if I had been adopted! I was so unhappy about her knowing so much more than I did. Even though my sister felt horrible about what I'd overheard, she said I had to ask Mom and Dad.

So one day I drummed up the courage to ask Mom. The color drained from her face, but she wouldn't give me any information. Mom simply said that I needed to talk to my dad.

I'm guessing Mom put a bug in Dad's ear because the next day, Dad asked me if I wanted to go fishing for a couple of days. Apparently, Dad and I would have a man-to-son talk during this weekend trip. This is what I got: "Son, I know you must have a lot of questions, so if you want to talk, I'm here." That was all my dad said.

I didn't think it was my place to ask questions. I felt it was his responsibility to tell me. After all, I was the kid; he was the dad. A few months later, my dad and I really talked about my emotions and how what he had done to our family over-whelmed and infuriated me. We cried together, and through his sobs, my dad asked me to forgive him. I did, and I can tell you that offering that forgiveness allowed me to release a lot of anger.

Now, decades later, as a man with a family of my own, I am beyond grateful for my parents' decision to stay together and heal their marriage, and for the forgiveness and compassion they demonstrated as they did so.

PART THREE:
RENEW

12

A New Perspective

IT WAS A LATE FALL EVENING, *and I was enjoying time at home with our about-to-be-adopted baby girl, Mia, our special gift from God. She was four months old and had been with us for only thirty-three days, yet she had already started changing our world in ways we could never have dreamed. Ron was on a business trip that weekend while I stayed at home to care for our new baby.*

I was preparing for bed, having settled Mia down. I remember being so excited that Ron would be home the following day. Just as I crawled into bed, the phone rang. I wanted to go to sleep, but since I recognized the number, I answered it.

I looked at my watch—11 p.m. No one ever called me that late, so it had to be important. The caller was a friend who also happened to know the "other woman."

"Are you okay?" I asked.

"Yes," she replied, "but something has been bugging me all day, and God is not letting up until I follow through."

She had seen "the other woman" at the school their kids attended and had asked how things were going. "The other woman" replied that it hadn't been easy, and things had taken a bad turn financially since she and her husband had separated. Even so, she was determined to keep her kids in that private Christian school. The school was trying to help by paying her to house a foreign exchange student. She had also taken another part-time job—her third one.

My heart sank. It had been five years since our friendship had ended. In that moment I realized how much I had missed her and her kids. It was devastating to think how she was still paying a huge price for having the affair. She had lost her marriage and was now a full-time working mom with three young kids to raise and no family unit or partner to help her.

She truly was alone. Neither the woman nor her husband had any family in Vancouver. Our family had been the closest thing they had to family-like support. My heart was breaking as our mutual friend continued to share the story. She ended by saying, "I don't know why I felt you should know, but I couldn't get it out of my head all day!"

Even though my heart was filled with compassion, I couldn't figure out why God would want me to know all of this. What was I to do with this information? I was finally able to sleep, but it didn't last long.

I woke at 3 a.m. Unfortunately, this was a "God wants me to wake up and stay up" moment. I have had a few of those nights before, and each time I've asked God the same question: Can't this wait until morning? *Each time the answer is the same, and it's never been favorable. So that night I didn't even bother to ask. I wiped the sleep out of my eyes and started to pray. I knew immediately what I was supposed to be praying about, and thankfully, God was quick to share what He wanted me to do.*

I was not prepared in any way for what I felt God was telling me, not because I didn't want to do it, and not because I felt I couldn't do it, but because I thought what God wanted me to do would be a slap in the face to my husband. He had worked so hard to forgive himself. Now I was going to tell him that I wanted to bring "the other woman" back into our lives.

On that night, God asked me to help take care of her children financially. The situation certainly wasn't the children's fault. They were victims who once had a two-parent, secure family home and were now being raised by a single working mom with three jobs, visiting their father on weekends.

I reasoned that God just wanted us to help, that's all. We could help with their school fees. That wouldn't be too much to ask, right? God was clear on what He wanted me to do, but not so clear on how to serve this up to Ron. After about an hour of trying to figure it out, I fell back to sleep.

When Ron returned from his trip the next day, I knew I needed to tell him what had transpired between God and me. Let's face it: There isn't a good time to tell your husband that you and God want to pay "the other woman's" bills. This was going to be horrible.

"Ron," I said, "I need to talk to you about something very serious."

"I have something serious to talk to you about too," he replied.

"Really? Okay, you go first."

He quickly responded with, "I'd rather not—you go first."

So I went first, with my eyes looking down at the blanket that covered our bed, telling him everything that had happened, from the phone call at 11 the night before to God's wake-up call at 3 the next morning.

"What time did you say God woke you up?" Ron asked.

"Three in the morning. Is that the only question you have to ask, after everything I just shared with you?"

"Yes," he responded, "because that would make it 6 in the morning back East in Baltimore, and that was when God told me I needed to take some monetary responsibility for the destruction of a family."

Talk about God's amazing sovereignty! Ron told me his answer to God was that he'd do whatever he needed to for the wrong he'd committed, but that he didn't want to put me through any more heartache. He then asked God to speak to me if this was really what He wanted him to do.

We looked at each other in disbelief, and then hugged and cried.

The next day I called the school to pay for the children's tuition. The school called my old friend with the great news that someone anonymously had paid for her children's tuition for the year. The next day, I received a message from her. She knew in her heart it had to be us. And that is how our friendship began again. Over the next year, we saw each other periodically and began to rebuild a friendship that has lasted to this day. Once again, she has been there for me through many difficulties, especially at the time of my husband's death years later.

Please understand that reconciliation with "the other woman" or "the other man" is not at all common or encouraged. If your spouse had an affair with your best friend, don't feel that you need to be reconciled with that friend. I'm not recommending that you try to reconcile. I included the story of our restored friendship, however, as another example of God's compassion and how He can make gold from the ashes of even the greatest fires.

That said, find a new way to look at your situation. God gave us a new perspective that evening, and He can give you one too. Seeing your situation through God's compassion will be the only way for you to overcome the monumental obstacle between you and healing.

There is no greater enemy to a marriage than the person who has stolen what only death should have the power to take: the body and soul of your mate. So how could I forgive my friend? And why would I *want* to forgive her? At first I didn't want to forgive her, and I wouldn't have been able to without God's grace and intervention.

Before I carry on, I want to reiterate something important: Forgiveness should never be optional. For your own emotional and spiritual health, you *need* to forgive. Notice I didn't say anything about the recipient. Forgiveness frees *you*. That's why I say it's not optional, not if you want to walk in freedom.

Notice that I didn't say *reconciliation*—I said *forgiveness*. My story is unique in that my friend and I did eventually reconcile, but as I stated earlier, this is not the norm. And please understand that you are not condoning sin when you forgive.

Compassion: Let's Review

The dictionary meaning of *compassion* is a feeling of deep sympathy and sorrow for another who is stricken by misfortune, accompanied by a strong desire to alleviate the suffering. You might react strongly to the words "stricken by misfortune" and think to yourself, *The misfortune has stricken me, not her/him!* The truth is, misfortune strikes everyone affected by infidelity. In my particular situation, all were hurt. Everyone in our circle sustained damage in some way.

It's been said that hurt people hurt people. My first reaction to the affair was not compassion and, I'm sure, neither is yours. It's human nature to want to cast the first stone, especially when the person has been caught red-handed. When people are guilty, we want justice to prevail. We want them to pay for what they've done. We instinctively want the perpetrator to suffer, and only then can we rest assured that all will be right in the world again. It's not in our nature to love unconditionally and to forgive those who hurt us. But thank God, we're *not* God! And thank God, He doesn't always give people what they deserve.

It would not be fair to assume that if you have compassion and offer forgiveness, everything will work out just fine. That is not true in every case and might not even be true in most cases, but right now we are focused on your case. In your case, it could be true!

But even if your marriage isn't reconciled, you'll need to make the decision to forgive, just as Jesus chose to forgive those who beat Him and crucified Him. If you choose to hold the grudge, you will be the one to suffer. You simply cannot be free while holding onto anger or resentment.

Science has shown that holding a grudge against someone who has wronged us, which is the biblical definition of unforgiveness, actually creates toxins that roam around in our bodies and make us physically sick. Neuroscientist Caroline Leaf, the author of *Who Switched off My Brain?*, says research indicates that "75 to 98 percent of mental, physical, and behavioral illness comes from one's thought life."[1] The antidote to most of those toxic thoughts is forgiveness, so don't—at any cost—make forgiveness optional.

To forgive, I had to change my perspective and not see my best friend as "the other woman" caught in adultery; I had to see the woman I knew. I had to see my *friend*: the one who had stood by me, helped me with my kids, laughed with me, and cried with me.

Of course, I understand that the one who has betrayed you may not be your friend or someone you know. Thank God for that, because it means the infidelity was one betrayal, not two. The point is that changing your perspective can be the tipping point to forgiveness, and once forgiveness falls, you can start to effectively renew your life.

Most of the counseling and group work I do with couples focuses on helping betrayed spouses see their betrayer differently. A couple who attended one of our weekend workshops finally found freedom and forgiveness when they both realized something important about the husband's past. He had been sexually abused as a child by a male babysitter, a trauma that set him on a path of self-destruction. He sought the approval of other women outside of his marriage. When his wife saw the sexual abuse listed on her husband's story-board, she was filled with compassion instead of anger. She was finally able to move from seeing herself as the spouse who was "never enough" for her husband to seeing his truth and empathizing with a man feeling forced to prove his man-hood to cover the shame of the abuse.

Healing cannot happen if we are not willing to see beyond the hurt and anger. Your end goal is to live life in freedom and better than you ever have before. The exercises in this book offer you practical ways to begin the healing process, starting with the smallest shift in your perspective. Changing your viewpoint will bring great freedom for the betrayed and the betrayer.

The Woman Caught in Adultery

Before we talk more about adjusting our perspectives, I want to share with you the story of a woman whose past I'm inti-mately familiar with. This woman had been leading worship in her church for more than a decade. Her enthusiasm for music and worship was evident in everything she did, and everyone she encountered could see her passion. She would spend many late nights preparing for Sunday worship and productions, and her team was excellent under her leader-ship. She and the team's coleader seemed to have the right chemistry to make it all work. As a result, every song, every transition, every note led to higher worship.

It seemed like a perfect match, until she felt the first inappropriate feelings toward her coleader. That's usually the time to flee, as the Bible warns us. Instead, the woman nurtured those feelings, which led to compliments and a shared desire to spend more alone time together "just to talk." Not much more needs to be said. We all can guess where this story ended: in a full-blown affair.

When the affair was discovered, both couples had to face the horror of a public dismissal. No help was offered, but rumors ran rampant and the pain became almost unbearable for them both. Several years after the affair, the woman's husband moved on.

For years, this woman lived in shame and remorse until she was able to find a little church where the response to her story was mercy instead of condemnation and ridicule.

When I hear stories like these, I think back to the friend who betrayed me and how she was treated so unfairly. Church members were downright cruel to her and her children. No one offered help to them when her husband left.

Our human minds want to tell us that people who hurt us somehow deserve whatever negative consequences come their way. When my mind starts to drift back toward that well-worn path of "They deserve this," God usually directs me back to the story in John of the adulterous woman caught in the act. No one in the angry mob surrounding her thought she deserved mercy. In fact, the law of the day stated that she could and should be stoned to death.

But Jesus chose to see her heart through His love and His Father's compassion instead of her sin. Not only did Jesus forgive the woman, refusing to throw even a pebble at her, but He caused her accusers to walk away too. How did Jesus get the Pharisees to change their perspective on this situation?

Let's look at John 8:3-11 together:

The scribes and the Pharisees brought a woman who
had been caught in adultery, and placing her in the
midst they said to him, "Teacher, this woman has
been caught in the act of adultery. Now in the Law,
Moses commanded us to stone such women. So
what do you say?" This they said to test him, that
they might have some charge to bring against him.
Jesus bent down and wrote with his finger on the
ground. And as they continued to ask him, he stood
up and said to them, "Let him who is without sin
among you be the first to throw a stone at her." And
once more he bent down and wrote on the ground.
But when they heard it, they went away one by one,
beginning with the older ones, and Jesus was left
alone with the woman standing before him. Jesus
stood up and said to her, "Woman, where are they?
Has no one condemned you?" She said, "No one,
Lord." And Jesus said, "Neither do I condemn you;
go, and from now on sin no more."

How did Jesus, by writing in the sand, turn an angry
mob around and cause each of them to drop their stones?
It's evident to me that Jesus softened their hearts toward
this sinful woman by turning their attention toward
themselves.

The best part for me was what happened next: Jesus
looked the woman in the eye and helped her see that all her

accusers were gone and He was the only one there. Imagine this woman facing her certain death that day. One moment with Jesus changed everything! Because of Him, she had a new life.

When Jesus said that He didn't condemn her, His forgiveness was *immediate*. But I'm sure the journey of healing and walking in that forgiveness was a process. The woman was offered a life of no shame, but she had to walk it out by going and sinning no more. It was up to her to leave the shame behind. Both she and the accusers learned something new that day. The lesson of the writing in the sand was clear: We must examine ourselves before hurling stones at our enemies.

As much as we would like to believe the Pharisees were nothing like us, we must admit that they demonstrated at least one good quality: their honesty about their sinful behavior. When Christ said, "Let him who is without sin among you be the first to throw a stone at her," a genuine hypocrite would have thrown stones regardless. But these quite-human-yet-sometimes-heartless Pharisees did not. From the oldest to the youngest, they all left. They are to be commended for holding themselves to account. Do we really want to be the ones to cast the first stone?

How easy it is to judge others, but what character it takes to actually love our enemies. Loving our friends is easy. Saying "Praise the Lord" when things are going well doesn't take much effort, but what about when life changes for the worse? What then? What do you do? Where do you go in your head and heart? When the dust settles, does your heart harden, or do you surrender to God so He can soften it? Do you ask Him to give you His eyes to see and His ears to hear?

A new perspective is worth its weight in gold. That new way to see my situation allowed both my husband and me to grow, heal, and renew our marriage. Only when I was able to see the affair from a side other than my own was I able to take action and heal. That healing led to the best years of my marriage by far. That's why I can confidently say that it was "the other woman" who saved my marriage.

After the long and hard process of restoration, we came to the place of renewal. I was able to fully give Ron my whole heart and the one thing that I knew he needed most—nurture. I was no longer withholding it from him. I was safe to give that to him. And for the first time, we were truly intimate because we were one.

True love and forgiveness do not keep score. They rely on God, who can take what was meant for evil and turn it around for good (see Genesis 50:20). Do I wish the affair had never happened? Of course! Would I go through the two most painful years of my life again? Absolutely—because what resulted were the best twenty years of intimacy with the true love of my life!

Renew Exercise

R3: Renew is the last step in your journey to freedom and restoration. Imagine an old house with the roof caved in, the walls broken down, the door falling off its hinges: You won't be able to piece it back together using old materials. You can try, but sooner than later it will fall apart again. Nailing a new board with an old rusty nail just won't do the job. In order to have a livable dwelling, you're going to have to roll up your sleeves and rebuild.

To renew means to have a new perspective. Can you look at the broken-down shell of a building and see an amazing house? To renew is to rebuild. It's restructuring the way you see things, the way you react to things, and the way you perceive things. Renew is not only a renovation of your thinking, but it's making your mind-set better than it was before.

Every day, challenge yourself to see the truth about yourself and your relationships through God's perspective. Renew your knowledge, as it says in Colossians 3:9-10: "Do not lie to one another, seeing that you have put off the old self with its practices and have put on the new self, which is being renewed in knowledge after the image of its creator."

Take a moment to actually visualize how God sees you and your relationships. Perhaps Psalm 139:14-16 will help you understand what God thinks about you:

> I praise you, for I am fearfully and wonderfully
> made.
> Wonderful are your works;
> my soul knows it very well.
> My frame was not hidden from you,
> when I was being made in secret,
> intricately woven in the depths of the
> earth.
> Your eyes saw my unformed substance;

in your book were written, every one of them,
    the days that were formed for me,
    when as yet there was none of them.

Stop.

Breathe.

Pray.

Close your eyes and let God show you what He wants you to see. Continue daily to renew your mind by memorizing Philippians 4:8: "Finally, brothers, whatever is true, whatever is honorable, whatever is just, whatever is pure, whatever is lovely, whatever is commendable, if there is any excellence, if there is anything worthy of praise, think about these things."

Continue your journey of transformational forgiveness by not taking offense easily. Proverbs 19:11 says, "Good sense makes one slow to anger, and it is his glory to overlook an offense."

The next time someone says or does something offensive to you, ask yourself, *How can I change my perspective and see this person with eyes of compassion?*

For example, if you are waiting in line at the market and someone cuts in front of you, ask yourself about his or her history. What might have happened in this person's past to make him or her act this way? What could have happened to this person today? Maybe she needs to get home to a sick child. Maybe he's distracted because he doesn't know if he has enough money to pay for his groceries. It takes deliberate decisions and practice to *slow down* so you can see people through eyes of compassion.

As you begin to view everyone around you through eyes of compassion, your entire worldview will be transformed! The power to renew your future is yours as you carry out the R3 Factors of *reveal, rewrite,* and *renew.*

13

Living above the Line

WE HAD MADE *the decision to do whatever it took to heal our marriage, so off we went to Dallas, Texas, to attend a marriage seminar. We were about eighteen months into our healing process. It was day three of this five-day workshop, and I was tired. I was "seminared" out, and I just wanted to go back to my hotel room and get some sleep.*

Unfortunately, there was still one more session. I looked at my watch—it was already nine-thirty at night! How could there still be another session? Hadn't I already learned enough for one day? How many more layers could those instructors possibly peel off the onion of my heart? Apparently I was about to find out. The leaders had nicknamed me "Rebel without a Cause," but at this point I had no fight left so I gave it my best shot.

They stuck a man in front of me and said, "Tina, this is your dad. Tell him what you needed from him and never got." All of a sudden, I was wide-awake. My heart started pounding in my chest, and I instantly welled up with tears.

I began to talk to "Dad," telling him how much it hurt when he didn't protect me and how the long months he would spend out of town working had left scars on me. I explained how my life at home without him left me feeling empty and abandoned, that there was absolutely no joy when he left.

Then, out of nowhere, the words "Dad, I forgive you" spilled out of my mouth. I can't express how I felt when that weight was suddenly and permanently lifted off my shoulders. I felt like my body had received some sort of cosmic supernatural energy . . . until they placed a woman in front of me and told me this was my mom.

My body tensed and my legs stiffened. I told this stand-in "Mom" that what I needed was a mom who actually wanted me, a mom who would have actually been there for me. I told her that I wanted a mom who was proud of me and who wasn't so hard on me. At that moment, the words "I forgive you" didn't come.

The exercise was designed to lead us to a place of forgiveness. The words simply poured out of me when I addressed my stand-in dad, but they were locked inside when I talked to my stand-in mom.

The coach tried to get me to feel softer emotions, but all I had was anger from the years of feeling as if I was never good enough. Just when I was about to give up on the whole exercise, God faithfully met me right where I stood.

I looked at my stand-in mom, and I saw her as a sixteen-year-old teenager. I saw this scared young girl standing in front of me, holding her tummy and rocking back and forth. I could hear her saying, "Not now, not now. Please, God, not now!" I realized the truth: She was not rejecting me, the unborn baby inside of her; she was rejecting the loss of a special time that would never return. The teenager I saw wanted time to revel in being a girl married to the prince who had rescued her from her incredibly hard and complicated life. He had taken her to ball games, bought her ice cream, and spoiled her. She had married her knight in shining armor, but now she wouldn't have time to enjoy their new-found life together—just the two of them. She was pregnant and would now have to care for a baby. Growing up, she had always been a "mom." She had cared for her three siblings beginning at age eight. There was just no escaping it—she would always be a grown-up without an adventure of her own.

Compassion and understanding flooded my heart. Within seconds I uttered the words "I forgive you" as tears ran down my face. I finally understood the true meaning of something called "Living above the Line." Never again would I become a slave to anger!

I adopted the slogan "Living above the Line" long ago, and at every Relationship Lifeline workshop, couples' retreat, or conference where I am fortunate enough to speak, I talk about "living above the line."

The "line" exists in each of our lives. It represents reality—how you really see and do life. Every day each one of us will make a choice: Will we live in the light, or will we walk in the darkness? If you choose to live above the line, in the light, then you choose to live as God wired you. He promised us life, and His Word even promises "life more abundantly" if we will seek His Kingdom first.

Conversely, by choosing to live below the line, you then live by the lies of the enemy, whose sole purpose is to steal, kill, and destroy you. But Satan can't destroy you if you don't give him access. Proverbs 4:23 says, "Watch over your heart with all diligence, for from it flow the springs of life" (AMP). God mandates that we guard our hearts. You give the enemy permission to mess with you every time you slip below the line.

Let me explain how our baggage triggers our decisions to live above or below the line. In the illustration, the first vertical line represents the *intention* you had when you first came into your relationship. On the day you said "I do," did you intend to follow the vows you made to love, to have and to hold, in sickness and in health, for better or for worse? You no doubt intended to follow those sacred promises. So what happened?

For Ron and me, the answer was simple: The rocks happened. Those heavy rocks crept into our lives and hardened our hearts. Unresolved issues of our past happened to be the type of rock that weighed us down and almost finished us off. When we carry unresolved issues in our hearts, we're putting ourselves in the devil's playground. His desire as your enemy is to keep you trapped below the line. Get out of there!

Christ has made you a conqueror. In fact, He has made us all more than conquerors. I once heard a preacher say that a conqueror is someone who wins a battle. People who are more than conquerors have *someone else* do battle for them. Jesus fought and won the battle at the Cross so you can "live above the line." He has promised to battle for us. Let Him!

Look at the line as your reality—the "what is" in your life. There are some things in our reality we can control and some things we can't control. What we all control are our mental, emotional, and spiritual reactions to that reality. This brings us to the second vertical line, which represents your *decision*. Every day you get to decide, *What am I going to do with my reality?*

We can decide to react to our reality in one of two ways: either by going above the line or by dropping below it. Whether we live below or above the line depends largely upon our decisions. Unfortunately, the *rocks*—the hardness of our hearts—get between our intentions and our decisions and cause us to stray from our original plan.

If we decide to live below the line, then we are choosing anger, resentment, bitterness, disappointment, shame, self-pity, unforgiveness, control, blame, guilt, vengeance, addictions, and so on. We will pay the price. However, if we choose to live above the line, we can live with joy, laughter, peace, confidence, passion, dreams, kindness, faith, forgiveness, acceptance, purpose, hope, strength, and, most of all, love.

The most important thing to realize is that we get to choose the life we will live. This is what renewal is made of. Living above the line is how you renew every day. When you choose to drop below the line, you are giving way to your fear, which is the root cause of those debilitating emotions and chaotic reactions. Opposite that fear is compassion, which will help you rise above any circumstance that may come your way and stay above the line.

You can't change your story, but you can rewrite and renew it! You were wired by God to live above the line with the love, forgiveness, and abundant life we were promised as God's children. Remember, though, in order to *rewrite* your story you need to face the line that represents your reality—and that reality needs to be dealt with. You cannot heal or change what you aren't willing to reveal.

But once you've revealed your reality, you can decide to live above the line—and I strongly suggest that you do. You'll only hurt yourself if you don't. Don't choose to make yourself sick by living below the line. Think about this Bible verse: "Unrelenting disappointment leaves you heartsick, but a sudden good break can turn life around" (Proverbs 13:12, MSG).

Give your heart a "sudden good break." You can change your life, and it starts with the decision that living below the line is where Satan wants you to live.

Consider my life: When I chose to look through the eyes of compassion, I was able to see past my own pain and realize that I wasn't the only one hurting. My heart had hardened from the pain I was living through, but compassion softened my heart. When that happened, I was then able to tear down those walls protecting me from the fear of any future pain.

Once I opened my heart to grace and forgiveness, I experienced the greatest gift I could have ever given myself. Admittedly, most of my life before that had been filled with the toxicity of living below the line. When I made the decision to rise above the line, everything changed for me. Even though I couldn't change my past, I could change how I reacted to life's challenges.

Just as I did, you may slip below the line from time to time, perhaps even multiple times throughout the day, but don't make your bed there. Don't get cozy there. Recognize what's happening and get back to where you want to be— *above* the line. I used to live, breathe, and sleep below the line. Occasionally, on a good day, I would visit life above the line. When I experienced forgiveness myself and began forgiving and offering compassion to others, my "bed" moved, and I never settled back under the line again. I will confess that on occasion I do visit my old "friends"—anger, resentment, guilt, and sometimes even "Woe is me." However, these days it's only a visit!

It is absolutely true that God can use all things—the good, the bad, and the ugly—and work them out for our good. Romans 8:28 says, "And we know that for those who love God all things work together for good, for those who are called according to his purpose."

How many times have we read that verse, but in the thralls of despair tossed that ribbon of hope out the window? However, when you make the decision to forgive, you can receive the same revelation I did—that not only is God's Word completely and emphatically true, it's alive and full of incredible, unexplainable power. Just as they did for me, God's promises will permeate your entire being. When I read His promises, I felt renewed and confident that I was going to make it!

Because I chose to live above the line through compassion and forgiveness, I knew that my husband and I would dream again, and that life could and would be better than it ever was before. I firmly believed that nothing could diminish God's promises of living above the line and the life He intended for me, our marriage, our children, and whoever would listen to our story. I didn't plan to have an entirely new revelation about my life and its significance at age forty-two, but it was certainly welcomed and sorely needed.

So when you consider your story, be encouraged about what God can do in your life and find strength in His Word: "Be strong, and let your heart take courage, all you who wait for the LORD!" (Psalm 31:24). "Have I not commanded you? Be strong and courageous. Do not be frightened, and do not be dismayed, for the LORD your God is with you wherever you go" (Joshua 1:9).

Living above the line caught on quickly in our lives, and subsequently in our classes. I remember a single mom of three children under age seven coming to one of our programs.

Her husband had left her and had refused to spend the weekend at our four-day seminar. As far as he was concerned, they were finished. His wife attended anyway, deciding that her personal health was worth the investment.

She worked harder than anyone there. She had a purpose. She knew that she was fighting for her three little children. She had started her healing journey and was determined to raise her kids in the healthiest way possible, even if that meant doing it as a single mom. She decided that everyone in her family would be doing life "above the line."

After she got home, she gathered her kids around the refrigerator, where she had placed the "Living above the Line" illustration. The drawing had a thick red line in the middle. The good words, including love, peace, kindness, compassion, and forgiveness, were above the line. The sad, negative words, including anger, control, unforgiveness, envy, resentment, and defensiveness, were below the line.

She explained the meaning of living above the line to her kids as well as the consequences of not living above the line. She told me later that she was astounded at how well those little children took to the concept and how differently they started behaving. The children began to live above that red line and would even remind each other when they were slipping below it. I had to laugh when she shared with me what her youngest child said to her one day: "Mommy, you below the line!"

Identity Thief

There's a thief we need to guard against in our lives, but we don't always see him coming. We're often like the homeowner mentioned in Matthew 24:43: "But know this, that if the master of the house had known in what part of the night the thief was coming, he would have stayed awake and would not have let his house be broken into."

We may not see him coming but we know his intent, described by Jesus in John 10:10: "The thief comes only to steal and kill and destroy. I came that they may have life and have it abundantly."

The thief meant to kill and destroy me. But God actually caused me to look up and understand that He intends to give me abundant life above the line. I traded my "stuff" below the line and made a decision to start "living above the line"!

Unfortunately, sometimes we have a hard time letting go of the emotions that fall below the line because we think they're protecting us. Let me explain. If I'm using anger to protect myself and make me feel strong, I might be afraid to let go of that anger. *What will happen if I let go of it?* I wonder. *What will protect me and make me strong?*

The only way to let go of the familiar emotions below the line is to look above the line and reach up for the healthy emotions: joy, love, peace, forgiveness, and kindness. God intends for you to live above the line where dreams, purpose, and abundant life reside.

Is God's intention for you worth the struggle to get past the rocks in your life? Jesus always lived above the line. Jesus did everything that His Father told Him to do, and He did it while being moved with compassion. He is our example. He gives His children their lawful birthright of compassion. But even a birthright must be accepted. You *get to* decide if you will let compassion into your life. It's your choice. (More on this later, but those three little words "I get to" would become Ron's legacy.) Forgiveness comes from the power of compassion. Compassion is the driving force behind living above the line. You *get to* decide if you want to live above the line or below it.

Ask yourself, *Where do I live most of the time? What percentage of time do I spend above the line and below the line?* Do you spend 80 percent of your life above the line and only 20 percent below the line?

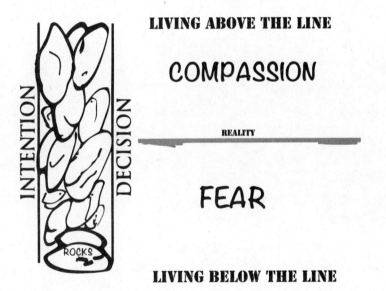

LIVING ABOVE THE LINE

COMPASSION

REALITY

FEAR

LIVING BELOW THE LINE

INTENTION

DECISION

ROCKS

Living above the Line Exercise

Complete the chart above. Your decisions cause you to exist either below or above the line. When your personal rocks are triggered and your buttons are pushed, what kind of decisions do you make? Write down your toxic thoughts and reactions below the line.

Next, make the decision that resolving the past will produce your best life—living above the line. What could be above the line if you choose to live God's way? Write those things above the line in the chart.

14
I Get To . . .

It was a Saturday morning *in March, and the weather was beautiful. Both Ron and I were in a spring-cleaning kind of mood. I had been complaining about the closets and thought some decluttering would be in order. Ron wanted to get at his garage.*

I have to admit I'm not much of a spring-cleaner; my idea of spring-cleaning is moving. (Which we've done a lot!) But it was one of those days when Ron couldn't stand stepping over the clutter in his garage anymore. So we finished our morning coffee, gave each other a kiss, and got to work.

About an hour into filling bags of giveaway clothing, I started hauling the bags into the garage. I carried the first two bags to the other side of the garage door and proceeded to walk back upstairs for the next two. Only this time as I opened the door to throw in my second set of giveaway bags, I got a killer look from Ron. But he didn't say anything, so I quickly made my third trip. This time when I opened the door I was greeted with a bark.

"What are you doing?" Ron said.

I responded with the same tone. "I'm cleaning the closets, and I didn't even bother you to carry down my heavy bags!"

Ron was not impressed with my logic. "Really, Tina, you have no respect for the space I'm trying to clear in here! I didn't create a clean path for you to reload it with your stuff!"

Oh, *I thought to myself,* the fight is on. What a man thing to do, making this all about respect! *I spun around with no response—he hated when I just walked out—and slammed the door as I walked back into the house. I barely took two steps when I did a 180 and stomped right back out to the garage. I glared at Ron and yelled, "By the way, you get to clean this garage. Do you know why?"*

He looked shocked and asked, "Why?"

"Because you have a garage!" I said. "Remember, you always teach that the alternative is imagining not having a garage to clean!"

We looked at each other and burst into laughter. Well, that was that. Smiling, Ron said, "I'm sorry, Babe!" We finished our day with clean closets and a clean garage.

———— ◆ ————

Once Ron got sick, he had what could only be described as a God-breathed epiphany. One day he woke up and proclaimed to me and anyone else who could hear him that from now on, no matter what, he would *get to* . . . He would *get to* live another day. He would *get to* love another day. He would *get to* breathe in the sweet aroma of the flowers in our garden, my perfume, the smell of his favorite food. From that day until his last, my husband lived that. "I get to" weren't just words for him—they drove his every thought and his every action. He lived a handful of years following this decision, and I can personally attest that his enthusiasm and pure joy in "getting to" not only changed his remaining years but continues to change all of ours as well.

This powerful phrase can transform your attitude about life, too, and help you live above the line.

Let me explain by telling you about a seminar I facilitated in 2017, about three and a half years after Ron passed away.

The seminar is a four-day event that gets deep quickly. It consists of ten- to twelve-hour days that drive participants to their emotional core so they can learn how to *reveal, rewrite,* and *renew* their stories.

It was the evening of day two, and the R2: Rewrite session was about to begin. In the seminar, rewriting explores the arena of forgiveness. This would be the first "forgiveness circle" our participants would experience. The forgiveness circle is as simple as it sounds, except for people who are hurting, angry, and/or bitter, it is anything *but* simple. The larger group breaks up into several individual small groups and forms a circle. Then, with the help of a facilitator, participants are asked to extend forgiveness to someone who has hurt them. Forgiveness is not only taught but also experienced in and through this process. It's experiential in nature and is incredibly moving and effective. The goal of the forgiveness circle is to coach the participants to express who and what it is that hurt them and how it made them feel.

This is where the real work of a good facilitator comes into play. An abundance of sensitivity is key. Facilitators have to be aware of the energy and "feel" the circle. They need to know when to step up and when to let things go. This is also where we as leaders rely heavily on God to do His work through us so that we can effectively lead our participants to their end destination: compassion.

The exercise is effective if people fully commit to it. When they recount how their hurts have affected them and then move toward compassion, it allows God to help them rewrite a negative story into something powerfully positive. Remember, you can't rewrite the facts, but you can change how you feel about them. One of the goals of *rewrite* is to see one's story from a new and different perspective so that each person can turn his or her toxic thoughts and feelings around. That is *rewrite* in a nutshell. It's taking the power of the feelings that have owned you for a long time, consistently taking you below the line, and turning them on their heads.

We were finishing our second evening, and everyone in the group was feeling the high that comes from experiencing the freedom of forgiveness . . . everyone, that is, except one young lady. The facilitator working with her tried everything, yet every trick in his proverbial facilitator's handbook— including asking the woman to view the person who hurt her so badly as Jesus might see him—failed to produce the desired effect. No matter how much this woman seemed to want to forgive, she was not able to get there. It was late and everyone was tired, so we released the class for the night.

The next morning, we started early as usual, but the smiles on the faces of those who had achieved the wonderful freedom forgiveness brings made the long night worth every extra minute.

To start the session, we gathered all the small groups together and had a few people share about their experiences the night before. Some of the participants looked physically different after their experiences. True forgiveness is so powerful that it can, and often does, change someone's physical appearance. People tell us they have actually been asked if they've had "facial work" done after attending one of our seminars.

The second person to share with the group seemed like a walk-in—I honestly didn't recognize her. By day three, I usually know everyone's face pretty well, but I couldn't place this woman. That changed when she started to speak.

She began by saying, "I left feeling very distraught and upset last night because I could not forgive my father. I went to bed without the energy to even remove my makeup or get my pj's on. I just threw myself on the bed, feeling defeated, like I had failed at something else. Then, while I was lying flat on my back in bed, a surge of weird power came over me. Suddenly, alone in my hotel room, I heard a loud voice yell out, 'I don't have to forgive; I *get to* forgive. I *get to* forgive my father!'"

She finished by saying something even more amazing: "I felt like that man, your husband, who I don't even know, spoke those words with my voice. That was it! Done! I forgave my dad just like that. I literally sat up in bed feeling like I had just dropped a hundred-pound weight."

After hearing her story, it dawned on me how powerful the "I *get to*" message really is. I knew it was powerful for my husband. If he said it once, he said it a dozen times a day.

The "I *get to*" message enables us to make choices and

choose what is right. "I *get to*" is a way of life that switches our victim mentality into a victor's perspective. When we say "I *get to*," we realize that we have the power to make the decision to be compassionate and believe that there is good to come from trusting that God's grace is sufficient. We might be weak, but He is strong, and we *get to* rely on His strength.

Don't be ashamed of your weakness. In 2 Corinthians 12:9 the apostle Paul said, "But [God] said to me, 'My grace is sufficient for you, for my power is made perfect in weakness.' Therefore I will boast all the more gladly of my weaknesses, so that the power of Christ may rest upon me."

In the end, if you rely on God's strength, then He will get the credit and you will have a life-changing testimony to share. My testimony and my husband's testimony have changed thousands of lives, and more importantly to me, many of those were children.

When Ron and I came to the place of knowing true forgiveness in our lives, we realized that we don't *have to* forgive, but we *get to* forgive. I especially realized that I don't have to live in darkness and bondage; I *get to* live in freedom and compassion. Whether the other person deserves it or not, I deserve to be free. When I forgave my mother in 1992, I got a taste of what it was like to be free, and there was no way I was ever going back to bondage!

If you let it, those three simple words will change your life. Not in a silly you'll-win-the-lottery kind of way, but in a profound daily-attitude-change-for-the-better kind of way. If you allow it, that phrase will color everything you say and do, and that change lived out will influence everyone you encounter as you walk through your daily life. I can't express how drastically that phrase changed my life as I saw Ron live it out. He was the most grateful man I ever met. That's not to say every day was wine and roses. Trust me: For him and for me, it certainly wasn't. But those three words allowed us to change our perspective when the situation seemed dark. That phrase allowed us to see the light behind the clouds, the sun behind the rain, and the rainbow behind the storm, and for that I will always be grateful to my man.

R3 for Life

It was my daughter *Jenny's high school graduation, and we were about to walk into the auditorium when I received a call from my mother, who was in Australia. I answered the call, "just in case." The problem was that I stayed on the phone, knowing there was no pressing issue or urgent matter that needed to be addressed. Meanwhile, Ron just stood there, fuming. He kept prodding me to get off the phone, but I just couldn't imagine hanging up on my mother. Once we finally got to our seats, I reasoned, No harm; no foul. We hadn't really missed anything, right?*

What I failed to realize was that as our eighteen-year-old daughter had walked in moments earlier, making her way toward her designated seat, she saw that the only two empty seats in the auditorium belonged to her mother and father. She was crushed. Her embarrassment at having to watch her parents walk in late and take their seats might have been dwarfed only by her thoughts of what might have happened to make us tardy. How late would her "perpetually late" mother be? Or worse, had we been in an accident? The only reason I could offer was an inconsequential conversation with my mother, which made Jenny feel she was playing second fiddle yet again.

Ron knew that I had no boundaries in place when it came to my family.

———————— ◆ ————————

My lack of healthy boundaries with family members was the last wedge in our marriage, and Ron and I would need the R3 process to get past it. We learned that the R3 process isn't a onetime procedure but more of a lifelong relationship strategy. Keep that in mind as you make your own journey through the reveal, rewrite, and renew process.

We came face-to-face with our need for R3 again after our second move to California, which happened about ten years after the affair. We were in an awesome place in our relationship, but this particular move had a major effect on our marriage.

At that point, I had no idea how to resolve my unhealthy lack of boundaries with my family and adult children. This was the last rock or, more to the point, the last gargantuan boulder keeping Ron and me from going deeper in our relationship, which was something we both desperately wanted.

Ron felt he couldn't compete with family, so he had given up trying. He forced himself to accept that this was a part of me that would probably never change. Unfortunately, sometimes we think we are doing well if we decide to simply accept something. But if it's only a surface acceptance, one that lives in our heads, our hearts will grow hard as resentment starts to take over. Hardness of the heart will eventually kill any relationship. This is exactly what was happening to Ron, and neither of us had any idea what effect this was having on us until we moved to California and gained some distance from my family.

Writing this now, I'm reminded of so many couples who live in a constant state of turmoil over their in-laws. I've heard about epic battles that ensue at the mere mention of so-and-so coming over, or even the news of a conversation that occurred with so-and-so. After twenty-plus years of working with married couples in conflict, it's easy for me to see why every nation around the world has in-law jokes. A husband once asked me, "How do I get my wife to stop running to her parents every time we argue, and how do I get her parents to stop getting involved and always making me the bad guy?"

Here's what I told him: It is imperative, especially when you are in the midst of a deep, emotional disagreement or fight, that you not run to family, friends, or confidants who are going to be negative about your marriage. These relationships are amazing resources given to each of us from God, but they can also be your marriage's worst enemy. So tread lightly, and beware and be aware!

In my own situation with family, a destructive codependency was creating deep resentment in my husband, even though he thought he was "handling it"! I had always felt so responsible for everyone, not only in my family circle but with my extended family as well. To be honest, I felt a deep-seated need to fix not only *everything* I thought needed fixing, but also *everyone*. I would drop everything to meet urgent needs. It was "tyranny of the urgent" at its worst, and I was amazing at it.

Once we left our home in Vancouver, we both felt this huge release, and that's when the stronghold of resentment that Ron had unknowingly carried for years, resentment that had been secretly destroying our marriage, reared its ugly head. Once I could see this demon, it became not just Ron's issue; it became something I could work on. It's impossible to work on something you can't see, won't acknowledge, or just flat-out ignore.

And you had better believe I did work on it. I was embarrassed to have been so blind to something that was now so staggeringly obvious. This is a perfect example of how change, even a seemingly insignificant one, can reveal a world previously hidden.

The coolest part of this new revelation and my absolute desire to change was that it created a freedom that Ron and I hadn't felt before. It made us both feel like newlyweds who were collectively building a family unit. *Collectively* is the key. We had been raising a family together before, but we always felt like two separate entities who were at odds, simply because we were unaware of the problem or unable to articulate it.

Now this issue was out in the open and being dealt with . . . one step at a time, one rock at a time, one breath at a time. That's how you heal, and that's how you rewrite your current story.

Our ministry in southern California began to flourish. We had become a sought-after resource, and we spoke in some of the largest churches in Orange County. People were being set free. Families were being restored. Marriages were being saved. And all the while, we were living the dream. We played. We raised our little girl, Mia, who was four when we moved to California. (We had adopted Mia during our Canadian days of turmoil and struggle, but that's a book for another time.) We rode bikes and went for walks on the beach. Ron golfed. I laid in the sun. We worked hard and played hard. Our life was so good it was almost cheesy. Moving to California for the second time and letting go of my codependent behaviors was healthy and part of the renewal process for Ron and me. Even though ten years had passed since the infidelity in our marriage, the process of renewing my heart, my thoughts, and my actions was relevant and ongoing.

We realized that the R3 process of *reveal, rewrite, renew* was not a onetime event. It was a paradigm that we would live by for the rest of our lives. The same can be true for you if you embrace the process and take it with you on your journey through this life.

The R3 system is not a weekend, a seminar, or a once-in-a-while thought. Just as nurture and care are the backbones to marital success, R3 is a transformative guide that, when truly embraced, will lead you both to a better marriage and a better life. But the information about R3 in this book won't help you unless you actually use it. Healing is intensive and not for the faint of heart; it requires you to make a decision and a commitment. It takes determination. Remember, R3, like marriage, is not a destination; it's a lifelong journey.

During our marriage, God graciously provided Ron and me with many healing opportunities. To take advantage of those opportunities, we needed to step out in faith, trust in His goodness, and reveal our fears as we jumped into the unknown. Had we any idea of the next "unknown," we would have both crumpled to the ground, probably never to get up.

16

Heartbreak Hill

IT WAS A COLD *December Sunday in 2009, ten days after we received a life-changing phone call letting us know that Ron had cancer. Ron and I had made our way back to Vancouver from California to receive medical treatment, and on this particular day, Ron had risen early to get ready for church. I felt like I'd been run over by a train, so I remained in bed and pulled the covers up around me.*

I had no desire to go to church. I didn't have the energy. I wanted to pull the blankets over my head, bury my face in the pillow, and hope this was all another one of those awful nightmares. I silently begged God for anything that could help ease the pain—for a promise, a sign, anything I could hold onto. God, please give me peace. Tell me he isn't going to die. *I closed my eyes, and a stream of warm tears began to soak my pillow.*

My mind drifted back to the phone call we'd received back in California from Ron's doctor.

"I suggest you get home to Canada right away. This is life and death."

I'm sorry, what? He has what? He's only forty-eight. He's in the prime of his life. He's not even sick.

"I'm so sorry, Mr. Konkin. You have cancer."

The word cancer *had reverberated inside my head. How? Why? You have to be kidding? Here I was, again on the end of the phone hearing the worst news I could imagine.*

Unfortunately, the doctor wasn't kidding. A new chapter had begun that day—one that lasted four years and ended with the death of the man I loved more than life itself. Sometimes life gives you a right hook that knocks you to the mat. In less than thirty seconds, my incredible "California Dreamin'" life had come to an ugly, grinding stop.

So as Ron dressed for church that cold Vancouver winter Sunday, I lay in bed, my head still spinning with the news and my heart still breaking as worry engulfed my entire being. Even though I prayed for peace and for God to promise me this would turn out all right, I still struggled with the thought of giving control of the situation to God. I wondered, How can I give this up to God if He didn't stop the cancer from forming in the first place?

As I had in so many circumstances before, I finally realized that I didn't have a choice. There was nothing I could do, so I acknowledged that God was in control. I needed to trust and believe; I needed to put my faith in action.

———— ◆ ————

In 2008 we had made the decision to move to Orange County, California, the home of Disneyland and one of the richest counties in the nation. Everyone there seems to be bathed in golden sunlight with a perpetual "magic hour" glow. The dark side is that Orange County is brutal on marriages and actually claims a staggering divorce rate that has climbed to a shocking 72 percent; that statistic is for *first* marriages, never mind second and third tries.

Orange County had a different effect on us. We had never imagined life—let alone our once-broken marriage—could ever be this good. To top it off, being back in full-time ministry was not only fulfilling but now carried a new sense of purpose for Ron and me. We were living the dream until that phone call came—and the timing of the call couldn't have been worse. It came on day one of a four-day counseling workshop, during a ninety-minute dinner break. Broken couples gathered after the break, with no one knowing the news we'd just heard. Ron had determined that he was not dying that weekend, so we would carry on with our mission of "healing relationships, one broken heart at a time."

It was Sunday evening, our work was done, and Ron and I began packing to return to our Vancouver home. At one point, we both paused and looked intently into each other's eyes. I studied the man I loved and admired for a long list of things, including his fortitude. I knew how anxious he was to get home, yet he seemed incredibly calm. On the other hand, I felt as if it was all I could do to hold myself together. Inside, I was screaming, crying, and banging at the imaginary walls that kept me from being able to do something, from being able to help. I wanted, with every ounce of breath in my lungs and every beat of my heart, to make the diagnosis go away. I wished for that giant eraser once again. This time I would erase this horrible new reality.

My gaze remained fixed on Ron's eyes, and that seemed to anchor me. I knew that we were going to have to come to grips with our new reality, and I also knew that we would be forced to apply every lesson we had ever learned and every teaching we had ever taught if we were going to get through this. The question ultimately came to this: Were we going to focus on the disease, or were we going to focus on our destiny?

I've heard that sailors say if you find yourself caught in a fierce storm, it's best to set your sights on the horizon and not on the treacherous waters that are crashing about you. In our situation, I found it difficult if not impossible at first to see the horizon, much less focus on it. As soon as we returned home, we were bombarded with more news from doctors telling us that there was no treatment, no cure, no hope— Ron had only four to twelve months to live.

I realized that if I was going to hand control to God during this journey and not lose my mind, I would need to get myself in shape spiritually. I would need to become *spiritually* strong. Among other things, I would have to resist the temptation to quit the ministry we had spent decades building.

Facing Our Heartbreak Hills

I want to share a powerful message that greatly influenced me during this trying season of life. It held me up when I felt myself slipping into despair; it still holds me up today, and I hope it will encourage you, too, as you face your difficult journey.

The message was about the race the apostle Paul spoke of

in 1 Corinthians 9:24. Paul is clear that we all have a race to run; he is equally clear that only one person wins. Don't misunderstand me when I say "one person wins." Our spiritual race is not against other runners but against the forces that want us to quit. We are not competing with each other—this is a personal race. How are you going to win *your* race? That is the question.

In his message, the preacher compared our race with the Boston marathon, but not in the way you might think. Everyone knows how grueling it is to run twenty-six miles in this particular competition and how much training is necessary if a runner desires to win. What most people don't realize is that runners have nicknamed different sections of the marathon to indicate the terrain of that part of the course. That night the pastor spoke on a section of the course dubbed "Heartbreak Hill."

A *Runner's World* article by Robert James Reese titled "Just How Bad Is Heartbreak Hill?" describes the difficulty of this stretch.

> We've all heard the horror stories about Heartbreak Hill; it is perhaps the most notorious of all elevation changes in major marathons. . . .
>
> But elevation change isn't the only thing that makes a hill tough; the rate at which that change happens also makes a big difference. The climb late in New York City as runners enter Central Park may have a touch more in the way of elevation gain, but it's spread out over twice the distance, so it doesn't seem nearly as hard. In fact, when you compare

the grade of the biggest hills of the five marathons, Heartbreak is the steepest at 3.3%.

The final thing to consider is the point in the race at which the hill comes. Heartbreak Hill comes after runners have traveled over twenty miles, much of it on grueling downhills that wear out the quads. So, even if the hills near the start of Marine Corps and Los Angeles are bigger, they don't seem as bad because of where they are placed.[1]

Let's see how this race compares with the race of life. First, the sudden elevation change makes Heartbreak Hill notoriously difficult, and sudden changes can also make life especially challenging. I know this from personal experience—the discovery of the affair and learning about Ron's cancer diagnosis were just two of the sudden changes I faced.

Second, by the time the runners reach the base of Heartbreak Hill, they have already completed a staggering twenty miles of the course! They must then face this final, steep incline. That scenario seems a lot like life to me. It's usually when you're already exhausted by difficult circumstances that you encounter a hill threatening to kill your spirit.

Don't Quit

Heartbreak Hill is appropriately named since it's where most runners lose heart and quit the race. Whatever you are going through, don't let your own personal Heartbreak Hill take you out. Once runners make it to the peak of Boston's Heartbreak Hill, they can hear the band playing and have only a half mile of downhill running to reach the recovery section.[2] Making it to the Boston marathon's finish line is worth the pain of climbing that final hill.

In Corinthians, Paul encourages us by saying that the finish line of life is also worth the hill we're struggling to climb. The joy you will have again is worth the ache of a treacherous incline. A band is waiting, and a recovery section is close by.

As long as we're on Earth, we're in a race where death is the finish line and eternity is the prize—that time where we will enjoy our Savior. Because of Ron's life-and-death battle, I would need to focus on a new strategy for running the race, one that relied on always following God's promptings and, as usual, running to win. My resolve would need to be firm if I was going to avoid the "woe is me" road and not curl up in a ball on the floor.

As long as either of us had breath, we needed to keep running forward, one foot in front of the other, all the while trusting that God would provide a way out. I knew that all the crazy, ugly thoughts I was having, the ones trying to wear me down and tempting me to quit at every turn, were from the enemy. He was trying to destroy my faith and steal my joy, peace, and laughter. Doubts and fear would quickly pollute any good thing that happened during the day.

I had to rest in the fact that God never promised us life would be a bowl of cherries or a sweet-smelling rose garden. What He *did* promise is that if we trust Him and continue to live in the promises of His Word, He will be faithful, and beyond that, He will be our ever-present help in times of trouble. He promised to help me endure this heartbreaking trial, but I had to resist the temptation to quit the race.

My friend, whatever you are going through, don't let the enemy overtake you with his lies. He's a master at deception, and his only objective is to trip you up and get you to lose faith and quit the race. Fight, my friend, because this is a fight for your life. Hang on to 1 Corinthians 10:13: "No temptation has overtaken you that is not common to man. God is faithful, and he will not let you be tempted beyond your ability, but with the temptation he will also provide the way of escape, that you may be able to endure it."

Conquering Heartbreak Hill

To conquer our Heartbreak Hills, we need to focus on God's promises as we persevere. We also need to train if we're to make it over the hill of our trials. And finally, we need to keep our eyes on the prize that's waiting for us on the other side of Heartbreak Hill.

Persevere

I remember watching an interview with a Boston marathon gold medalist. The runner was asked, "What hill was the most painful one? Just how painful was it?" The interviewer went on and on about the severe pain this guy had to endure to win this race.

The medalist answered, "It doesn't matter if it's at the beginning, the first hill, or the last. It doesn't matter if you're the first runner or the last runner. It doesn't matter if you quit halfway through, and it doesn't even matter if you make it all the way to the end without winning the gold. Every part of the race is painful. Your body is being tasked, it is being beaten, and every part of the marathon is pain, whether you are the gold medalist or you come in last. You've suffered pain."

The runner's answer tells me that pain is not the issue—pain is a given. It's the perseverance *through* the pain that matters most.

Ron taught me a lot about keeping our minds pure as we persevered. He made sure that we both stayed aware of any toxic thoughts trying to creep into our minds. Ron would fill his mind daily with God's promises, and those promises gave him confidence that God was in control.

As God has done for all of us, He determined the start and finish of Ron's race before he was even conceived in his mother's womb. Ron was confident that his life belonged only to God, but he also believed that his work was far from finished. Legacy became Ron's priority. Because he was acutely aware that what he did on Earth would live on long after he was gone, Ron was determined to leave a legacy that would positively affect not only his wife and kids, but everyone he had influenced through his work.

Ron's strong desire to live on through his work and life is where the "I Get To" campaign was birthed. No matter what burden you are carrying today, persevere. Whatever you do, don't let the enemy snuff out God's light and His precious gift of life. Stay in the race. Remember, you "get to" live another day! Make the most of it. Psalm 118:17 says, "I shall not die, but I shall live, and recount the deeds of the LORD."

Train

Ethiopians and Kenyans often win the Boston marathon's first three medals. Someone once asked the runners if they knew why. One of the Ethiopians said that Heartbreak Hill didn't bother runners from his country; in fact, they didn't slow down there or even breathe heavier. When asked why, the runner explained that the hill was just like their training ground in the mountains of their homeland.

They train for this race. What race are you training for? Are you training for Heartbreak Hills that might show up on your race? If you're training for an easy race by running a few flat miles per day or even less, you'll find yourself ill-prepared for the hills of a more complicated race. Are you striving to win the race, or are you simply in survival mode?

We are all called to run the race of life, and we don't know how many personal Heartbreak Hills we will have to endure. The reality is that the Heartbreak Hills will continue until we meet Jesus our Savior face-to-face. Only if we run the race to win and endure until the end—Heartbreak Hills and all—will we hear Jesus' words, "Well done, thou good and faithful servant."

If the thought of another hill exhausts you, I understand. If you think you've had more than your share of Heartbreak Hills, I want to tell you that you are not alone. Like the prophet Habakkuk, I learned that perseverance comes when we praise God and rejoice in Him no matter what life dishes out. We're not praising God *for* the circumstance or the hill we're facing; we're praising God for who He *is*. He has you in this!

> Though the fig tree should not blossom
> And there be no fruit on the vines,
> Though the yield of the olive should fail

And the fields produce no food,
Though the flock should be cut off from the fold
And there be no cattle in the stalls,
Yet I will exult in the LORD,
I will rejoice in the God of my salvation.
The LORD GOD is my strength,
And He has made my feet like hinds' feet,
And makes me walk on my high places.

HABAKKUK 3:17-19, NASB

Notice the word *yet* in the sentence, "Yet I will exult in the LORD." Do you have "yet" in you? Do you even know where your "yet" is?

That three-letter word bothered me. How could I possibly be asked to be joyful when my husband had just died, leaving me alone with a teenage child? How could I rejoice? Maybe a better question would be, *Why do I have to rejoice?* Here's why: God's Word says so.

In whom am I to rejoice? Certainly not in the death that has occurred, and not in the sickness, but in the God of my salvation, the One who holds all of humanity's hope.

And what kind of hope are we talking about? Hope, in Scripture, means a strong, confident expectation. Biblical hope stresses two things: first, that your future is secure; second, that hope is what you can't see but still believe in.

Even though biblical hope can't be seen, it comes with a sense of certainty and security. When our beliefs are Christ-centered, we can rest on what God promised us in His Word.

Is your marriage colored with biblical confidence?

Remember, you *get to* do life together. You *get to* heal together. You *get to* cry together. You *get to* fall on the floor together, and more importantly, you *get to* stand up together. It's easy to point fingers, to fall into a he-said, she-said, childlike back-and-forth battle. It's easy to be offended and place blame, but hope says *forgive*. We're not competing against each other, except maybe in the desire to be selfless.

In sporting events, struggles and obstacles stand in the way and must be overcome in order to win the prize. In our spiritual life, there are similar challenges, things we need to overcome if we are to win the prize. How are we to accomplish this? How do we run the race well and win the prize? Hebrews 12:1 provides an answer: "Therefore, since we are surrounded by so great a cloud of witnesses, let us also lay aside every weight, and sin which clings so closely, and let us run with endurance the race that is set before us."

We need to lay aside *every* weight; in other words, throw off everything that hinders us. Everything! What is weighing you down? It's easy to see that a drug addict needs to get rid of the drugs. But what about the person who continually works fourteen hours a day? Why don't we tell him to get rid of the extra hours so he can spend time with his family? Or what about the guy or gal who is "doing well" but hasn't seen his or her kid's ball game or dance recital in years? What "weight" are you prepared to give up to receive healing in your marriage?

Athletes train. They have to. What are you doing to train for *your* race? Athletes also need to know the rules, or they risk being disqualified. The race we are running also has rules, and we also risk being disqualified if we are ignorant of them or just decide to ignore them.

Focus on the Prize

Athletes are committed to winning, and they speak of the prize as their primary motivation. You also have to keep the prize in the forefront of your mind; otherwise, how can you make a day-to-day plan of action?

Paul says it like this in 1 Corinthians 9:24: "Do you not know that in a race all the runners run, but only one receives the prize? So run that you may obtain it." That's excellent advice: See the prize and run toward it.

Jesus ended his earthly race by suffering on the cross, which brought Him a crown of joy. The joy that was set before Him helped Him endure. You won't be able to endure the race of your life and its challenges—the problems in your marriage, the loss of a job or a house, or other circumstances that might lead you to despair—unless you keep your eye on the prize.

Most times we face Heartbreak Hill without a cheer-leader, and we have to encourage ourselves to keep going. If only we could see what's on the other side of our own personal Heartbreak Hill, we'd get through it. What's on the other side of your Heartbreak Hill?

The prize, if you choose to run your race to win, will be a new life with joy regardless of the outcome of your mar-riage. I would love to promise you that making it over your Heartbreak Hill will guarantee a new marriage, but I can't. Nobody can.

But I can promise you something else, because God does. If you run to win, if you focus on your relationship with God and then yourself, God promises you peace, joy, and most importantly contentment. Of course, if both spouses choose to enter the race together and are committed to running to win, the reward can be unexplainable joy in your marriage.

That's just how our God works. He uses our Heartbreak Hills for our good if we will only trust Him and persevere.

My prize is that I get to stand here today, right in the center of my calling, running my race to heal the brokenhearted. I don't know how many children's lives have been positively affected because I refused to quit our counseling ministry. Refusing to let the Heartbreak Hills on your journey take you out of the race has a ripple effect. Persevering is what counts, and those who have trained for the race, who've put in the miles and felt the pain of growing, will make it over Heartbreak Hill.

Remember, your journey over Heartbreak Hill is not only about you. Your DNA will be passed down to your children. What you model, they are likely to follow. Are you passing down a willingness to run the race for the ultimate crown, or are you modeling a race that leads only to an earthly crown that, in the end, counts for nothing?

My heart goes out to those of you who are in the midst of a marital crisis. If your situation looks hopeless, or your spouse has walked out or refuses to communicate, my prayer is that you will find a way to believe that God is a good God, all the time. He has already walked in your future, and He wants you to heal, no matter the outcome of your current situation. He wants to renew you and your marriage, but it takes two people to heal a broken union.

No matter what, you can choose to embrace the process of healing and let God lead your next steps. Remember, we are not promised tomorrow, but we do have today, and I urge you to be fully present in the day before you. What helped me was choosing to find joy in at least one thing every day. Whether it's the sunshine, a phone call with a friend, or something else, choose one thing to be joyful about. Don't miss an opportunity to change your mental and emotional state. Remember, what you feed, grows; feed light and life, not negativity.

What do you want your life and marriage to look like? How do you want your children to act when they are older? Put those things before you as your "prize." Then commit to the race, train for it, and you will find the motivation to persevere and conquer Heartbreak Hill.

17

Let's Put It in Gear

THE R3 PROCESS *(reveal, rewrite, renew) and its long-term results hit home personally for me on a day I spent with my adult kids and their staff from Whole Way House, a Vancouver-based charity.*

Every August, Whole Way House hosts a picnic in the park for the men of the downtown eastside of Vancouver who may be homeless or have lost their way at one time in their journey. My children invite all the men and the charity supporters to enjoy a day at the park. We barbecue and focus on having fun. I'm always proud to be at these events, to watch how my kids give generously and with happy hearts to the less fortunate men of the city.

The event takes a lot of work. The silent auction fund-raiser requires months of preparation, the games need to be set up for the families to enjoy, and the food has to be organized to feed a huge crowd.

One year, to reward the hardworking staff members, my kids planned a day of boating off the coast of Vancouver. I went along with the grandchildren for what turned out to be a wonderful day of fun. Seeing my adult kids and their employees hanging out on the boat, enjoying their music, dancing, tubing, board surfing, and just having a great day made my heart jump a few beats.

That day made me think: What would have been different in my kids' lives if Ron and I had decided to quit on our marriage?

I was reminded of the years following the affair when we tried hard to spend as many weekends as possible with our children, making memories on the lake where we all liked to spend time together.

As I watched the next generation enjoying the fruits of their labors, I was reminded once more that because we chose to renew instead of replace each other, I was able to enjoy watching my own children make memories that would last a lifetime.

Internally, I was celebrating the legacy of healing that God so graciously allowed in our lives. He healed our broken hearts, and this day was a direct result of that healing, of that renewing, of that revealing and rewriting.

At the end of the day of boating, I watched as the life jackets were stowed away for the next adventure and the boat was prepared to be trailered. I watched with amusement and pride as Josh tried to teach his sister how to bring the boat in and safely drive it onto the trailer—a scene reminiscent of the ones years before with him and Ron. The day also reminded me of times Ron patiently taught Josh and Jenny how to drive the boat and how to be safe on the water.

On this day, Jenny looked at her brother and said frantically, "Hey, it's been a while since I drove a boat. You already made me drive while you were surfing out there, and now you expect me to drive this boat onto the trailer?"

I'm sure she felt out of her depth at that moment. But Josh encouraged her that she could do it. Their dad had encouraged them in the same way. This stuff is generational, which is why it is so incredibly important that you work on yourself and your marriage.

Josh talked Jenny through it, telling her how to hold the boat straight and focus straight ahead on the trailer. His encouragement, like his father's, made the task sound simple. Jenny put her hands on the wheel and tried to turn it, but nothing happened. Josh told her to go forward and "give it some gas," but when she did, nothing happened.

It was then Josh noticed that the boat was still in neutral. "Hey, Sis," he said, "you can't steer if you're not in gear."

You Can't Steer if You're Not in Gear

I believe the scenario from our lake day provided me with a message for you, and this is it: Stay alert and plugged in. Always engage in life to the fullest. Make it a habit to: Stop. Breathe. Pray. That is the only way to move closer to renewing your life.

How real is that truth? You can try to steer the boat of your life and point it forward, but if you're not in gear, you're going nowhere. If you stay in neutral, if you stand still, you will paralyze yourself in the pain that you are currently experiencing.

My friend, you can read this book over and over again, but if you're not engaged you'll continue to find yourself standing still.

If you are going to *renew* your life and your marriage, you need to do more than read this book, attend counseling, and go to church. Those things are meaningless if you are not participating. And as much as you'd like to on some days, you can't just sit at home and cry if you expect to move forward.

My daughter was sitting in the boat, hands on the wheel, foot on the gas. She was doing everything right; she was ready, but without being in gear none of the instruction and encouragement mattered. If you're going to *renew*, you need to get out of neutral. You'll have to put yourself in gear, and then you'll be able to steer your way to renewal.

I wish I could tell you that my daughter was successful on her first try at getting the boat loaded onto the trailer. She wasn't. Her brother left her side and stepped off the boat so he could direct her onto the trailer and secure the boat. After her first failed attempt, he directed her to back up and try again. She got a little fearful, but she kept her eyes on the front of the trailer, listening to her brother's instruction and watching his hand signals. She was confident that his smile meant she was doing well. When she finally succeeded, everyone screamed, clapped their hands, and congratulated her. Jenny let out a sigh of relief, knowing everyone was safe and that she had successfully completed her task.

My friend, you will also have setbacks. But it's time for you to do the work, to take action. The exercises in this book will help you "get it in gear" so you can start steering your life toward a renewed future.

That day on the boat with my children, grandchildren, and the staff of their charity would never have happened if, twenty years earlier, Ron and I had not made a decision to put our life in gear, look outside the boat, and focus on Jesus instructing us and helping us to straighten out. He promises to be with you and lead you to safety, but you have to take action. Don't let fear stop you; in fact, promise not to let *anything* stop you from steering that boat to safe waters.

There's a photo I show nearly every time I speak. It's a photo of our family a couple of months before Ron passed away. I show it because it portrays a legacy—his and ours. You see, if we hadn't made the decision to restore our marriage, some people wouldn't be in that photo. My son met his wife at the new high school he attended after we moved because of the affair, so *she* would not be there, which means my granddaughter would also not be there. (She and my other grandkids, who arrived after Ron's passing, are the joy of my life.) My youngest daughter, Mia (the reason I wake up every morning), was adopted from a refugee mother with PTSD who was seeking help in Vancouver. Ron and I wouldn't have been working together downtown and met this woman if we hadn't taken time to rebuild our marriage and our ministry, so Mia wouldn't be in the photo either. My son and oldest daughter wouldn't be helping the homeless and less fortunate men of Vancouver if we hadn't started that ministry, which has now helped hundreds of men transition out of homelessness and experience unconditional love and care.

But there's a photo I don't show: It's a family portrait taken at Ron's deathbed on December 24, 2013. I'm thankful every day for this photo. You see, I don't know if any of us would have been in that photo with him the day before he died—in his bed, in his hometown, with his entire family surrounding him—if Ron and I hadn't decided to reveal, rewrite, and renew our marriage, allowing us to leave a legacy of forgiveness. And as Ron took his last breath early on that Christmas morning, we *got to* lie with him, hold him, love him, and release him to heaven, the place where he was welcomed into complete healing and where he heard what he'd longed so deeply to hear: "Well done, thou good and faithful servant."

It's important to remember that all of your decisions matter—today, in the future, and until your time here on Earth is over. Even more important, remember that your decisions directly affect the quality of life your children will ultimately live. It's not my goal to save every marriage, though I wish every marriage could be saved; it's my goal to help as many people as possible become healthy. I believe if your heart is healthy, your decisions will reflect that health.

I hope that you will be encouraged to put your healing in gear, land your boat, and step out into a brand-new, better-than-you-could-have-ever-imagined-it-could-be life and relationship.

When Jesus asked Peter to step out of the boat (see Matthew 14), Peter did, and everything was great . . . at first. He was doing just fine, walking on the rough waters with his Lord, but once he took his eyes off Jesus, he began to sink. If that had been the end of the story—"Peter took his eyes off Jesus and then drowned in the raging waters"—then the story would be tragic and pointless. But that wasn't the end of the story. Jesus was still there, watching, waiting, and helping. He was there to lift Peter up, and together they continued walking on the turbulent waters. Moral of that story: Keep your eyes on Jesus, and not only will you *not* drown, but you'll be able to walk on the waters of your raging troubles. Believe it, because it is truly believable!

I'm so proud of you. You've made it through the many hard lessons I've shared. My hope is that you are getting stronger by the page, that your hope has returned, and that you are already figuring out how you can *reveal, rewrite,* and *renew*!

It's Up to You

Decide to put your life in gear even while you're still in a mess! Notice I said, "Decide to." You won't want to, but do it anyway. It might annoy you—do it anyway. Sometimes interruptions are God's stoplights.

Here's a story about why it's important to get back in gear as quickly as possible. You've seen throughout other chapters that God uses mundane things, seemingly simple annoyances, to perform some big miracles. Being in the right place at the right time is rarely a coincidence. Things we like to dismiss are usually the most relevant. Obedience to the "little" things brings some of God's greatest blessings directly into your path.

It was August 17, 2004, and I was in my downtown office in Vancouver, where we had partnered with the city to establish better, safer housing for the hard-to-house "problem" men. That particular morning, the Internet in my office wasn't working and I desperately needed a document printed. I ran upstairs to the social worker's office and asked if I could use her computer. It was supposed to be a three-minute job. Then we were interrupted by a phone call, and within seconds of answering she excused herself and stepped out of the office.

She returned shortly, and I could tell by the look on her face that the call had not been a good one. "There are some things I just can't make happen!" she said.

The call was from someone at another building where the social worker worked part-time. She explained that a single mom was about to be taken to the hospital and was begging her to take her baby until she was better. This woman was a good mom, the social worker explained, but she had no friends or family to help her with the baby, and it sounded as if she was suffering from postpartum depression. The social worker told me that although she felt sick at heart, she was a single, working woman and she couldn't personally help this mother. She had to call Child Services; the baby would be taken to a foster home.

Immediately, these words escaped my mouth before my brain could process them: "Let me be family or a friend so they won't take the baby."

The social worker's mouth dropped open. "Are you serious?" she replied.

I was *very* serious. We managed to get to the mother's home five minutes before Child Services arrived, just in time to pass the ambulance taking that mom to the hospital. I didn't even meet the birth mother! The social worker had told the mother that we could be trusted, and that was enough. The baby was quickly handed to me right there in the house before we were hurried out through the back door. Since we left with nothing but two diapers and a car seat, we had to stop to buy formula, more diapers, and clothes for this three-month-old baby.

So here's the deal: An obedient response to an "interruption"—a cry for help—produced a lifetime of blessing for my entire family and, I'm guessing, for our precious daughter Mia.

Mia's biological mom was actually suffering from PTSD because of trauma experienced in her youth. Once out of the hospital, it was determined she wasn't healthy enough to care for her daughter. Yet she retained full custody of her child, giving her the sole right to choose the adoptive parents. You guessed it: She chose Ron and me!

Also, as a double blessing, the building where this all began is where my daughter Jenny and son, Joshua, continued to work, ultimately establishing Whole Way House after Ron and I went on to establish our ministry called Relationship Lifeline. God's way is always better than our own.

Get in gear. Be sensitive to God's blessings. They sometimes masquerade as interruptions!

18

Building a Loving Legacy

RON COINED THE PHRASE, "I *get to*," and today all three of our children live by those three words. The phrase is never far from our thoughts and constantly reminds us that life is not a black-and-white still photo. Life is a moving picture that is meant to be lived in glorious color—bright, vivid, deep, engaging, saturated, messy color!

I'm thankful and feel incredibly blessed that my children proudly carry on their father's "I *get to*" legacy. His story and impact as a husband, father, son, brother, friend, and mentor to many will continue to affect generations for decades to come. His desire to live on, beyond his years here on Earth, was reflected in his last written message: "I shall not die, but I shall live, and recount the deeds of the LORD" (Psalm 118:17).

I asked all three kids to write about their father's legacy and how it has influenced them.

Jenny's Story

My dad's cancer was by far the craziest roller-coaster ride I've ever lived through.

The biopsies.

The test results.

The waiting rooms.

The surgeries.

The trial drugs.

The hopes.

The disappointments.

The fears.

All of it was really hard, but the one thing that remained steady in all of the storms was my dad's faith in God's good plan. It was awe-inspiring to see how even though he was bombarded with toxic thoughts daily, he was able to keep his eyes focused on Jesus. The song "10,000 Reasons" became his personal anthem. "Bless the Lord, oh my soul." Every single day.

"It's easy to bless the Lord when everything is going well," Dad shared in one of his powerful, life-changing, heart-blasting messages: "The kids are good. The wife is good. The house is good. The car's not breaking down. It's easy to bless the Lord then. That's easy, but what about when it's not going well? What about when your whole world is rocked? When you get the call that it's 'life and death'? When you lie on an operating table, hoping that this time they'll be able to get it all? When your eight-year-old daughter is sad because you can't go outside and play with her anymore? When you're rushed to the hospital in an ambulance in excruciating pain, and it feels like your heart is being ripped out of your chest? Or when they tell you the cancer has come back, and there is nothing more they can do? What about then? Will you bless the Lord then?"

He did.

I can tell you that throughout the entire journey, my dad modeled what it meant to trust in the Lord.

And I tried to follow.

When I was a little girl, my dad would tuck me in at night. Every night he would get me ready, scratch my back, and pray with me. Then he would ask me which Bible story I wanted to hear. The story of Shadrach, Meshach, and Abednego and the fiery furnace was my favorite. I was only four, but two parts of the story always stuck with me: the young servants' confidence in their Lord saving them, and their vow that even if God didn't rescue them from the fire, they would still not bow down to the king's idol (Daniel 3:16-18): "Shadrach, Meshach, and Abednego answered and said to the king, 'O Nebuchadnezzar, we have no need to answer you in this matter. If this be so, our God whom we serve is able to deliver us from the burning fiery furnace, and he will deliver us out of your hand, O king. But if not, be it known to you, O king, that we will not serve your gods or worship the golden image that you have set up.'"

My dad was very much like those young servants. He never gave up hope that God would heal him, but even while he was sick, he never wavered from praising God.

When he was first diagnosed, we were all in shock. It

was like a blow to the stomach. The wind was completely knocked out of me, and I couldn't breathe. At some points, I didn't want to breathe. My world came crashing down.

He was only forty-eight years old. He wasn't sick. He was young and healthy. He never smoked or drank; he didn't even swear, for goodness' sake. How could he have *cancer*? They didn't find it until it was already in stage four. I began the research, using every scientific journal I could find on malignant melanoma. It wasn't looking good. Clark level IV meant Dad didn't have long to live.

You know the story. He was determined to keep living and keep living on purpose, to promote healing marriages and relationships and broken hearts. And so he did. He kept changing his world, one heart at a time. But after those first four months, something seemed to shift. He was still alive, and he was beating the odds. He was still healthy and shocking the oncologists. It was at this time when his "I *get to*" message was born. He suddenly saw everything as a blessing. Every day he would say, "It's a good day," simply because he woke up breathing. He would also say:

"I don't *have to* sit in traffic."

"I don't *have to* clean my garage."

"I don't *have to* go to work."

"I *get to* do all of those things because I'm still alive."

My mom often tells the story of being in the midst of a heated argument with my dad, and while she was yelling at him about something, he would give this side smirk right in the middle of the fight. Of course, this would make her even angrier, and he would finally just smile and say, "I *get to* fight with you!"

This wasn't just a saying or a teaching that he tossed around; the phrase became my dad's way of life. Every time a complaint or a grievance or even an annoyance crept in, he would shut it down. Honestly, it almost became annoying.

He would remind us not to let the little things bother us. "Don't waste your breath," he would say. So have compassion for that person driving so slowly in the fast lane. Be kind to the lady in the checkout lane who is taking forever to purchase her items. Have patience when you have to sit in a hospital waiting room or lie on an operating table. Show kindness to nurses and servers and customer service agents. Be thankful for all the things you have. If you're stuck in traffic, be thankful that you have a car. Be thankful for money to be able to buy groceries. Be thankful for access to medical care, doctors, hospitals, and medicine. So many people on this earth do not have those things.

It changed us all.

If he didn't complain through all the "cancer stuff," how could we dare to complain about such insignificant things?

Building a legacy became his reality.

What am I doing today to build my legacy? How will I be remembered? What will people say about me at my funeral? Was I a life-giving person or a life-sucking person? Did I light up the room when I walked into it, or did the light come on when I left? Did I leave a mark? Did I make a difference? Or did I waste my time? My gift? My talent? Did I live on purpose?

My dad would ask, "Who do I get to be a lifeline to today?" He was always looking for every opportunity to give, to love, to witness. His love for Jesus poured out of him.

He would say, "Don't wait for a diagnosis to start living on purpose and building your legacy. You may not get that luxury."

We used to play a song called "Thank You" by Ray Boltz for the training assistants in Relationship Lifeline. When my dad passed, we didn't even have to discuss which song would be sung at his funeral. We all knew it would be this one. The song is a poignant, beautifully penned tribute to every Sunday school teacher who ever felt overlooked, to every offering given that did not seem significant, and, finally, to all those who have given themselves in service to the Lord wholeheartedly like my dad did. Their reward, like my dad's, will be great, and they will not only hear their Father say, "Well done, thou good and faithful servant," but they will hear the testimonies of countless others whose lives were changed for an eternity by their legacy here on Earth.

Josh's Story

As a husband and dad, I thank God for the legacy my dad left me: Even when we mess up, there is nothing we can do to lose God's love. God's love heals, and I learned that nothing is more important in a marriage than compassion one for another.

One of the first verses that my mom taught our four-year-old daughter, Scarlett, was Ephesians 4:32: "Be kind to one another, tenderhearted, forgiving one another, as God in Christ forgave you."

My dad might have messed up, but his mess became one of the greatest messages of hope for hundreds of families. He was the greatest man I have ever known, and I thank God often that He gave my parents the strength, compassion, and ability to forgive one another and keep our family together.

I will never know what life would have been like if they had split when times were tough, but I do know that I am forever grateful for my upbringing in a very healthy and whole home.

One of the strongest and most secure relationships in my life was with my father, and I continue to have a great relationship with my mother. I'm not sure that I would have been blessed with these same relationships if they had taken the easier road and split up our family. Thanks, Mom and Dad, for never giving up on your family. I *get to* continue to live out your legacy!

Mia's Story

(Mia was thirteen when she wrote the following words.)

From the time I was two years old, I knew and understood I was adopted and I always felt special. Sometimes I did feel different, but I knew there was nothing to feel bad about. God truly blessed me by providing me with the Konkins. I wouldn't want to have anyone else as my family.

My dad was always about having fun. He would say we "get to" have fun today. Wherever we were, he always wanted to have a good time. Every day was a good day for my dad. He really valued God's blessings. So I loved getting to have fun, going fishing, going to Disneyland, on car rides, to the beach, you name it. My dad and I were like two peas in a pod. He was my best friend.

When I was five, my dad was diagnosed with cancer. My dad was given months to live, but he fought and remained my father for four years. My dad passed away when I was nine years old and I hated God for taking him from me. Today I'm thirteen and I still think it's not fair that my dad is not here, but I *get to* heal from that pain. I let God back in my life. Like my dad told me, he will never leave my heart. I *get to* remember him.

——— · ———

Ron Konkin's legacy exists today through me, his children, and those he touched because of choices we made to restore our marriage twenty years ago.

Yes, I can say "the other woman" saved our marriage, but only because the crisis alerted us to our problems and we decided to work on them. We decided to apply the R3 principles to reveal yesterday, rewrite today, and renew tomorrow.

God can—and often does—use anyone and anything to ultimately create in us clean hearts and right spirits. Psalm 51:10 says, "Create in me a clean heart, O God, and renew a right spirit within me." It took "the other woman" to show me that my heart was hard as rock—not in every way, but in a way that the enemy could use to weaken my marriage. When I hardened my heart for fear of being hurt, I had also shut down the gooey, soft part of me—the tender, nurturing, gentle part of my heart that my husband desperately needed. I shut down the sweet, nurturing part of myself, and that cost me dearly.

If you will trust me one last time and give God permission

to reveal your yesterday, He will be there to help you rewrite your today and, I promise you, He will also renew your tomorrow. He is a God of second, third, and fourth chances, and He promises to give us life more abundantly. He wants to make your life and your marriage better than it ever was before.

He did that for me. He will do it for you.

Don't discount the decisions you're making today for a better tomorrow; I'm surely glad we didn't! All my love and prayers as you get to work. Nothing worthwhile is ever easy. This journey is no different. Now let's get to it!

Acknowledgments

This book would still be a thought in my mind if it were not for "the other woman" wanting our story to make a difference, to be used in some way to heal the hearts of victims of betrayal and those caught in the grip of adultery. I also have to thank her children for allowing us to tell our story of failure and God's redemption for the greater good. To her children, I am thankful from the bottom of my heart for allowing both my late husband, Ron, and me back in their lives. Without their willingness, this book could not have been written.

I want to thank my late husband, Ron Konkin, for his foresight. He knew that the enemy wanted to use our failures to destroy our family, but that God would use those same failures to save thousands of families. When it seemed inevitable that life would be cut short for him, Ron made me promise that I would never stop telling our story. He would whisper in my ear how God does not waste one tear, one heartache, or one battle! "Babe," he would say, "we won the war when you forgave me; that's the miracle!" Every woman and every man needs to hear that message of true forgiveness.

To my two eldest children, Jenny and Josh, thank you for having lived through the drama of those two very hard years of healing after Dad and I had failed as parents. Thank you for understanding true forgiveness and loving your dad and I through it all. Thank you both for staying faithful to Jesus. Mia, thank you for being the child of our later years and for blessing us with a great new beginning. You were our reward for being obedient to God by forgiving and renewing our lives.

I must acknowledge that sometimes, at least for me, it's easy to forget how God randomly inserts unlikely events and equally unlikely people in our paths, people who can often times leave us wondering, *What just happened?* It was at a Saturday night service at Friends Church when the lead pastor, Matthew Cork, asked me to join the team heading to India for a pastors' conference. He asked if I'd be interested in leading a marriage seminar for 120 pastors and their wives. My lips said yes, but by the time I got to the parking lot, my heart sank. I had no desire to go to India, and especially not at that time, just after my husband had passed away. Clearly God had other plans, because it was too late to back out. Here's the amazing, God-works-in-wonderful-mysterious-ways part of the story: I met Greg Smalley on that trip. We shared the platform and our hearts with this incredible group of pastors. Greg Smalley put legs to my dream when he pitched our story to the Focus on the Family team. Greg Smalley and Matthew Cork, I am now and will forever be grateful.

I must acknowledge my Focus on the Family editor, Julie Holmquist, for the great calm force she was in this process.

She made me feel like a hero and provided encouragement that this book was going to make such a difference to the hurting.

Last but not least, I want to thank a longtime friend, Jon Van Dyke, who would prefer to stay unnamed. But I cannot leave his name out. How do I acknowledge the many times he was the bridge over my troubled water during the last two years of this project? When I became overwhelmed, he'd encourage me to just write and not censor my story, saying, "I'll do the rest." That calm in my storm made this book possible. Shannon Van Dyke, thank you for letting your husband spend all those hours helping me tell my story and for the many lunches we had that distracted me for a while. Jon has been around Hollywood sets for more than thirty years, training animals for movies, and he used that talent well with me. He sometimes had to bring this animal back to focus on the present task. Jon, you warned me that you are a scriptwriter and movie director, not a book writer. But you are the best cowriter I have ever known, and by the looks of it, many seem to agree with me.

Notes

CHAPTER 7: GUARDING AGAINST A HARD HEART
1. *English Oxford Living Dictionaries*, s.v. "reveal," accessed December 7, 2018, http://en.oxforddictionaries.com/definition/reveal.

CHAPTER 12: A NEW PERSPECTIVE
1. Caroline Leaf, *Switch on Your Brain* (Grand Rapids: Baker, 2013), 33.

CHAPTER 16: HEARTBREAK HILL
1. Robert James Reese, "Just How Bad Is Heartbreak Hill?" *Runner's World*, April 14, 2013, www.runnersworld.com/run-the-numbers/just-how-bad -is-heartbreak-hill.
2. "The Course: Fun, Then Sweat, Then Heartbreak Hell," *Boston Globe*, 2006, Sports, archive.boston.com/marathon/course/stage4.htm.

About the Author

FOR MORE THAN THIRTY-TWO YEARS, Tina Konkin has helped heal the brokenhearted through her story of abuse and abandonment. Tina has touched thousands of lives by demonstrating that your past doesn't have to control your future. She is the founder and director of R3 Lifeline and facilitates the Relationship Lifeline and the Couples Retreat programs. Tina is a sought-after motivational speaker who engages, entertains, and inspires her audiences.

To register for a four-day Relationship Lifeline workshop or a Couples Retreat program, visit www.relationshiplifeline.org.

FOCUS
ON THE
FAMILY®

How God Used "the Other Woman" is one of our many offerings to help you Focus on Marriage. Discover ways to build healthy marriages grounded in biblical principles at FocusOnTheFamily.com

You *can* survive this crisis . . . and learn to thrive!

Tina Konkin was devastated when she learned her husband was having an affair with her best friend. How could this happen to a Christian couple who helped other couples repair their relationships?

In *How God Used "the Other Woman,"* you'll hear the author's amazing story of a redeemed marriage that led to a successful marriage-coaching program. Learn how, with God's grace and plenty of work, Tina and her husband were able to not only restore their marriage, but also make it better than it ever was before. Their relationship not only survived—it thrived.

As the Konkins rewrote their marriage story, they discovered tools that have since helped hundreds of other couples in crisis. If you've come face-to-face with betrayal, this book is for you. The author will show you how to put into practice the same powerful "R3 Factor" healing principles that she and her husband used:

- R1: Reveal the hurts of yesterday.
- R2: Rewrite your story today.
- R3: Renew tomorrow by making your relationship better than it ever was before.

Exercises throughout the book will help you walk through each step as you read about the author's own journey from shock and pain to renewal and joy. Let *How God Used "the Other Woman"* help you find hope for a new future and set you on a path toward healing today.

Tina Konkin, an internationally acclaimed leader and speaker on the topic of relationships, is the cofounder and executive director of Relationship Lifeline. She has facilitated hundreds of seminars for couples over the past 30 years.

ISBN 978-1-58997-987-1
Religion / Christian Life / Love & Marriage
US $15.99
51599

9 781589 979871   EAN

A Focus on the Family Resource Published by Tyndale House Publishers, Inc.